ARISE AND WALK

ARISE AND WALK:

The Christian Search for Meaning in Suffering

PAUL A. FEIDER

Fides/Claretian
Notre Dame, Indiana 46556

© 1980, Fides/Claretian
Notre Dame, Indiana 46556

Nihil obstat: Terry E. Place
              Censor librorum
Imprimatur: † William E. McManus
              Bishop of Fort Wayne-South Bend

Library of Congress Cataloging in Publication Data

Feider, Paul A.   1951-
  Arise and walk.

  Bibliography: p.
  1. Suffering.   2. Faith-cure.   I. Title.
BT732.7.F44   253.5   79-23622
ISBN 0-8190-0634-3

1803

Contents

Introduction

"I have come that you may have life, and have it to the full" (Jn 10:10).

Life is gifted to us by God. We seek to comprehend its meaning, its paradoxes, its ambiguities, and we try to understand what insights, what light, the God-man, Jesus, radiates on its meaning and purpose. The experiences of suffering that come from being broken, and the experiences of healing that end in wholeness are part of that precious gift.

Life is challenged at times by the suffering that comes from being broken, wholeness is disturbed, and there is need for healing or restoration. As a student of ministry, I have sought to be a part of the human healing process. In reflecting upon some visits to the sick, I struggled with the fact that healing of any sort seemed like a distant

1

possibility and pain was clearly a reality. Whether on my occasional visits to the hospital or through my work of entertaining in nursing homes, I was left searching for words to say to people who were suffering. I had to face the question: What hope, what comfort, what "good news" does the gospel offer to those suffering? That question, which stands at the roots of this book, prodded me to question the value of suffering, while at the same time to pursue the ministry of praying for healing. My continued searching along with new experiences led me to more questions. Should we expect healings to occur, or is such an expectation harmful to accepting sickness? Why are some people healed while others are not? Is faith the only missing element? Why does God allow sickness if he loves us? Does suffering have value and if so, should we ask for healing?

It is questions such as these that have prompted this book, not because some philosophical answers will put my mind at rest, but because these questions are being painfully pondered and felt in the minds and hearts of people in hospitals and nursing homes, churches and funeral homes every day.

Introduction

I pursue this project out of concern for these people and with the conviction that a closer look at scripture and the person of Christ will lead to some life-giving insights.

Suffering, and consequently healing, touches people in different facets of their person: suffering of the soul or spiritual suffering caused by sin; suffering of the mind or emotions, caused by childhood memories or broken relationships; and suffering of the body caused by accident or sickness. These areas are closely interrelated in the human person, and injury in one area affects the others as well. Brokenness or malady in any one of these areas may heal to some extent by itself. In this book, when I speak of healing, I am referring to the natural process of healing being accelerated, or made possible, or transcended through the encounter of another person. Most often I will be speaking of the effects of an encounter with Christ.

To begin this pursuit, I will investigate suffering in the life of Christ and how he may have interpreted it. Next, I will search out as closely as possible a pattern of healing in his lifetime. Then I will present how suffering and healing were a part of the church, and how, through church history, those two experiences came to be interrelated. Considering some present-day authors on suffering and healing, I would like to then suggest some viable understandings of those experiences, which might lead to a more complete ministry of restoration to wholeness.

CHAPTER I

The Sufferings of Christ

> Though he was in the form of God, he did not
> deem equality with God something to be
> grasped at, rather, he emptied himself and took
> the form of a slave, being born in the likeness of
> men (Phil 2:6–7).

Life is a beautiful, created gift but at times we
lose sight of that beauty. For a person experienc-
ing pain it is difficult to see the beauty, sometimes difficult to see beyond himself as one suffering. Suffering has a way of blurring our view
on life, shaking what might have been held as
meaningful. Each of us can probably recall a few
instances of intense suffering in our life where
pain shook our understanding of life's purpose.
The real world at such times, is the world of hurt,
and care comes most often through one who enters that world, out of love, with words of comfort.

Taking on Suffering

It is this coming to our world that Jesus enacted through the incarnation—a love agreement that moved him to become truly human and within this humanness to reveal divinity. His revelation of the Father is transmitted through the life of a Palestinian man who, "became like us in all things but sin." To understand that revelation, we might search to discover how Jesus responded to suffering.

The gospel leaves only bits and pieces of the life of Jesus, telling things that people would have remembered, the things that made him different. The ordinary life of this God-man seems to have been no better or worse than the commonplace crudeness of the Palestinian villager. John L. McKenzie describes that life in this way:

> Such things as primitive and crowded housing (or frequently no housing), substandard nourishment, a working day of twelve hours or more, a total absence of anything we would call amusement or recreation, a wardrobe of a cloak and a tunic, constant harassment by one's betters, day to day subsistence on the margin of destruction; these were the life of the villager.[1]

6

The Sufferings of Christ

Although these were ordinary conditions of this time, and as McKenzie points out, "the villager would not count them among his sufferings," they indicate the real implications of Jesus coming to dwell among his people. From scripture and contemporary literature of that time, it seems evident that Jesus accepted the ordinary hardships of that time. He seems to use no divine power to exempt himself from the ordinary conditions of nature and the interactions implicit in its relatedness. He emptied himself and accepted becoming a man with all that that entailed.

Jesus' experience of suffering became exceptional to that of a villager as he began departing from conformity to live out his calling. The suffering which came to him because of his commitment in life is most prominently recorded in the crucifixion narratives, but can also be traced between the lines of the gospel texts. To conceive of Jesus as being above the emotional pain that would have accompanied his death is not to let him be human. The gospels tell of an ever increasing rejection of Jesus by political groups and even by his own hometown people, a rejection that must have hurt long before the nails were pounded in. "That he was unfeeling at the knowledge that he was the object of a campaign of calumny is impossible unless people meant nothing to him."[2] Jesus' response to hostile groups (Mt 12:1–15; Lk 11:37–54; Mk 7:1–13; Mt 23:1–39) indicates that their accusations penetrated to the point of hurting.

The pain of loneliness would hardly have been foreign to anyone who accepted such a mission, especially when rejection came as near as one's own disciples. It is not a pleasant thing to know that there are people who are convinced that our death will make the world a better place, yet it seems Jesus carried that emotional strain quite alone, since even those closest to him could not understand the issues involved. His lifestyle, in its singleness and uniqueness, left few people who knew him well enough to share the emotional burden.

Meaning in Suffering

In the midst of the sufferings inherent in his mission as they became increasingly apparent to him, Jesus did not deviate from his goal, namely, to preach the kingdom of God. We can speculate as to how Jesus came to understand the hard

8

results of his work. Perhaps to get an idea of what he may have been pondering, it is necessary to look at some Old Testament understandings of suffering.

Father Francis Cleary outlines six attempts in the Old Testament to interpret suffering.[3]

1) Suffering was viewed as retribution, meaning that sooner or later the righteous God will reward the good and punish the evil (Amos 5:14; Dt 30).

2) It was seen as disciplinary, making one strong (Prov 3:11).

3) In Habakkuk 2:4 suffering seems to be a probationary measure demanding patience.

4) Suffering in Hosea and Jeremiah was interpreted as revelational, enabling the prophet to enter into a deeper knowledge of God.

5) Most explicitly found in Deutero-Isaiah was the explanation that suffering had a sacrificial efficacy, it could help another person or group of people, e.g., the Suffering Servant.

6) Suffering was also viewed eschatologically by some who held that the more intense the suffering of Israel became, the closer they were to the divine inbreaking (Dan 7:13–17).

9

These understandings of suffering were influential at various times and in various groups throughout the Old Testament. The idea of suffering as being a punishment for the sins of the people was the most comprehensive understanding in the orthodox doctrine of Israel, but after the return from exile the idea grew that suffering was a punishment for individual sins. Ezekiel was the first to apply this doctrine, teaching that "the individual during his lifetime was to be rewarded or punished for his own behavior, not for that of his parents or nation."[4] This explanation found contradiction in everyday experience when the just suffered (e.g., Job), which eventually led to the concept of reward and punishment after this life. Though this understanding of suffering was present at the time of Jesus, he does not indicate an identification with Job.

Another response to suffering is the idea of vicarious suffering, suffering willingly endured for the benefit of others. This concept came out of the postexilic times, finding expression most concretely in the Suffering Servant songs of Deutero-Isaiah (Is 42:1-4; 49:1-7; 50:4-11; 52:13-53:12). Though this image is drawn from the deep and rich Hebrew tradition, it never achieved domination in Israel. "It was the favorite image of some of the smaller splinter groups like the Essenes, as the Dead Sea Scrolls have revealed."[5] Though it can be shown that a messianic interpretation of the Suffering Servant image is very old, that association was almost lost by the time of Christ.[6] The writings of Deutero-Isaiah were gradually covered over by more popular notions of a religious nationalism with hopes of salvation from the oppressing enemies of Israel by a powerful kingly messiah. The idea of vicarious suffering was not popular at the time of Christ, nor was it completely absent.

It is clear that the early church came to understand Christ's suffering as vicarious, as necessary for their salvation. It is more difficult to determine whether Jesus consciously identified himself with the Suffering Servant of God as a means of finding purpose in the suffering which he endured.

After evaluating the synoptic texts, Joachim Jeremias concludes that Jesus probably thought of himself as the Servant of God as described in Deutero-Isaiah. He points out that in general, "Is 40ff. had great significance for Jesus' sense of mission, cf. Mt 11:5 and par.; 5:3f.; Mk 11:17; Lk 4:18ff."[7]

More specifically he finds a number of passages where Jesus refers the servant sayings from Deutero-Isaiah to himself (i.e., Mk 8:31 and 9:12—Is 53:3, the servant must suffer much; Mk 9:31 and par.—Is 53:5, be delivered over; Mk 10:45 and Mk 14:24 and par.—Is 53:11-12, for the salvation of many; Mk 14:8—Is 53:9, be buried among criminals, without anointing; Mk 14:61 and par.—Is 53:7, and accept all this without opening his mouth).

While some of these passages may be wholly or in part the interpretation of the early community, Jeremias finds substantial evidence to support their antiquity and thus a higher probability that they came from the lips of Jesus himself. These references which identify Jesus as fulfilling the suffering servant role are older than any hellenistic influence. Some find expression in what Jeremias calls the bedrock traditions, such as the eucharistic narratives. Most convincing perhaps, is the fact that in some cases these sayings are so anchored in the context that they cannot be later additions. Jeremias writes, "This is particularly true of Mk 8:31 which is inseparably related to the sharp rebuke of Peter in 8:33; but the description of Peter as Satan cannot have been put on the lips of Jesus later."[8] Such evidence indicates that

Jesus was aware of impending death and probably searched to comprehend that event.

In agreement with the evidence of Jeremias and the conclusions of other sources,[9] I conclude that Jesus found meaning in the suffering stemming from his mission by identifying himself with the Suffering Servant of Deutero-Isaiah. Though the life of the Servant was filled with rejection, he was confident that his mission would end in glory through his death, a confidence that may have been quite encouraging to Jesus.

It seems very possible that Jesus resurrected the somewhat hidden notion of vicarious suffering and the connection between the Suffering Servant and the messiah. If indeed this image was "so lost that no one else could see the messiah in this stance,"[10] namely, as a suffering messiah, then we could understand the disciples' and even the early church's struggle to comprehend that connection. Aside from that theological connection, it is possible that the followers of Jesus were amazed by his actual acceptance of the suffering stemming from his mission and only slowly comprehended his particular reaction to the unpleasantries of his proclamation. In that light it would be understandable why Jesus had to silence those who did not accept the suffering that went along with knowing him. "Not accepting the full consequence of Jesus' being the Son of Man, Peter rejected the passion (Mk 8:30–32) and had to be silenced (Mk 8:33)."[11] Mark, in his gospel, three times reveals the disciples' rejection of Jesus' suffering or his prediction of it and three times described the inadequacy of such attitudes: Mk 8:33–9:29; 9:35–10:3; 10:42–45. His response to suffering may have been new—at least it was other than most people would have considered normal—and it was a part of the mission.

Summary

Jesus lived with the ordinary happenings of the Palestinian villager. He experienced suffering because of his mission, which did not deter him from his goal of preaching the kingdom, but in which he found meaning based on the Hebrew bible. Perhaps most significant is that he is the first to give manifest credibility to the notion that suffering can have salvific value, not in and of itself, but placed upon it by the free decision of a person enduring it for a purpose. It seemed to be important to him that people experience the value of his decision to endure suffering before they proclaim him as the anointed of God.

Ironically, perhaps, a significant part of his mission was to relieve the sufferings of others.

CHAPTER II

Healing in Christ's Life

> One of them, realizing that he had been
> cleansed, came back praising God in loud
> voice... Jesus took the occasion to say, "Were
> not all ten made clean? Where are the other
> nine?"... He said to the man, "Stand up and go
> your way; your faith has been your salvation."
> (Lk 17:15,17,19).

If we look closely at the gospel texts it seems
evident that Jesus responded differently to the
sufferings stemming from illness or the grip of
evil, than he did to the sufferings inherent in his
life mission. While he was willing to endure the
pains accompanying the proclamation of the
Good News, he was not willing to let sickness
and evil tear away at those he met—at least not
for those who sought healing.

Background Awareness

In attempting to discover what Jesus' response was to the suffering within others, we might look at some of the numerous healing accounts in the gospel. Since our knowledge of the healings of Jesus often forms the basis for our understanding of healing, it is important to try to determine exactly what occurred when Jesus encountered a sick person. To take the healing stories literally, without considering the historical setting, or the point that the author is trying to make, may leave us attempting to understand or exercise a healing ministry in a way that would have been foreign to Christ himself. Jesus' healing ministry is evident in numerous accounts, but it is also evident that the authors used these incidents to say certain things to their particular audience beyond just the healing event, or that they wrote the story in a form very similar to other healing stories of the day. A basic readiness to understand these influences might help us arrive at a more adequate view of how Jesus healed.

It is not possible to extract all the layers of theology that surround the healing stories, but

17

we might at least try to be aware of some possible influences on a particular healing story. We should try to separate the healing incidents which Jesus did around A.D. 30 from what the authors of the gospels might have been trying to communicate in recording a particular healing for the people of A.D. 70 or 80. Through comparing one gospel writer's account with another's, when this is possible, we can get some insight into what the authors added to the healing stories which were part of the early oral tradition. Matthew, for example, likes to amplify Jesus' workings more than Mark or Luke. On a couple of occasions, where the parallel texts of Mark and Luke have the healing of one man, Matthew reports the healing of two (Mt 8:28f.; 20:29f.).

By noticing the context of a healing story, what stories precede it and follow it, or the accompanying narrative, we can also get a hint at what the writer might be trying to accent for his readers in relating a certain incident. In the healing of the man with the withered hand (Lk 6:6–11), for example, it is evident that the main point is the controversy with the Jewish leaders as to whether it is lawful to do good on the Sabbath. The healing stories as reported in the gospels are intricately intermingled with Jesus' teaching and flavored by the author's arrangement of them.

Though an awareness of the different accents written into the healing miracles leaves us less sure of the exact details of a healing incident, it leaves us certain that some very significant encounters took place in Christ's life which changed the lives of people around him and were important to Christian believers many years later. It is difficult, and sometimes impossible, to determine how the evangelist has interwoven the historical events with his faith and the situation of his time, but if such a process was indeed part of the actual recording of the healing accounts, then the effort made to distinguish and understand that process can only enhance the message.

It might also be helpful for us, in looking at the healing texts, to realize the world view of that time period. The contemporaries of Jesus probably saw many more "miracles" in daily life than present day people would concede, mainly because they were aware of fewer explanations for daily happenings. Throughout their history they had come to "see God working" in very natural ways. An awareness of their world view does not eliminate the healings that Jesus did. It might help us to recognize that what the gospels describe in an almost magical way may have occurred in a way more similar to the way we experience less intense healings, namely, through an encounter with someone who shows a genuine love for us.

Their understanding of sickness and disease was related to their understanding of sin and demons. Their tradition would have led them to see the work of demons as the basis of certain human behaviors, such as mental sickness, leprosy, and seizures. Jesus responded to these kinds of human behaviors with apparently the same understanding of demons as Jewish contemporaries, yet within that understanding his encounter effects a significant change (Mk 9:14–28 and par.).

Physical sickness and physical disabilities, such as blindness and lameness, became very closely associated with a person's moral conduct or their parents' conduct. Judaism went so far as to ascribe a particular fault or sin to each sickness. From certain of the healing accounts concerning physical disabilities or illnesses, there are indications that Jesus saw a relationship between some people's moral life and their physical health (Mk 2: 1–12). From the reports of discussions concerning whose sin effected a certain illness (Jn 9:1–3), there are indications that Jesus moved away from a strict cause and effect relationship between sin and sickness which was prevalent at this time.

It is within these explanations of demons and sickness that God's power was made manifest. That does not limit God's power only to such understandings, though it may cause us to have to translate the constant manifestations of God's love and power into terms that allow ourselves and others to "see" and "encounter" him in our own world understanding.

Facts about His Healings

As we attempt to understand the healings of Jesus' life, it seems necessary to think through some of the facts about Jesus' healing ministry.

It is apparent that the healings of Jesus to some extent were his personal response to the sufferings of others. He was "hostile to what made people sick."[12] He is described in the earliest accounts as rebuking the illnesses that were directly attributed to possession by demons (Mk 1:25, 5:8; 9:25). He is spoken of as confronting and eliminating inner suffering that seems to stem from evil overpowering the life of an individual.

Jesus' response to suffering was not, however, a general elimination. John L. McKenzie writes:

> Jesus has no quick cure for suffering, and he does not promise a world in which there will be no suffering... Nor does he present any rationalization of suffering; after the gospel, as before, suffering is still one of the great irrational factors in human life.[13]

Jesus does not eliminate the suffering that was part of his mission. His life suggests a way of living with it. He does not eliminate all the inner suffering that results from human weakness, nor does he flee from the reality of its existence, but to those who did approach him open to his power, he provides a way to health. His concern for the people he met is evident in the miracle stories. "These are, almost without exception, accounts of how Jesus dealt with individual existing problems of suffering."[14] His life indicates a desire to eliminate the inner sufferings of people whom he personally encounters. It is through his person that he meets and eliminates specific instances of suffering.

Jesus does not remove all suffering, but when he does remove it, often it is in the larger context of liberating a person on a deeper level. Contrary to some of the pagan healings of his time, the primary or essential thing is not the removal of bodily suffering. Jesus' saving actions involve the liberating from suffering on all levels of the persons who came to him. From his Hebrew background, Jesus would not have thought of saving just the body or just the soul. He would have conceived of a person as one, interrelated, inseparable unity. "His redemptive concern necessarily encompassed the whole man."[15]

While Jesus seems to move away from the strong tradition of an illness being the retribution of a specific sin, he does not completely separate sickness and sin. Often Jesus concerns himself with liberating people from the sufferings that flow from sin. In many cases he tries to do this by first bringing physical healing and then moving on from that point (Mt 8:1ff; Lk 17:11ff.). Sometimes Jesus speaks words of forgiveness and then

23

follows up with external healing (Mt 9:2 and par.). The healing accounts indicate Jesus' desire to free people from suffering, but when that suffering is physical, Jesus' healing encounter seems to push beyond the physical level to free the person from the inner destruction of fear and guilt in order that they might arrive at a broader perspective of health, i.e., salvation (Mk 10:52; Lk 17:19; Jn 5:14).

Jesus' healings differ from the nonbiblical healings in that he does not heal for fame. At Epidauras, healing was done with some view toward bringing fame to their sanctuary. "Jesus regularly refused to do miracles either to save himself or to accredit his mission (Mt 4:1ff. and par.; 12:38ff. and par.)."[16] There are indications that Jesus' reputation spread, but not because of his active effort to have it so. In a similar way Jesus will not use his miracles of healing to cause sensations, as can be seen especially in Mark's accounts, perhaps with some of his own stylization, but hardly without some historical basis.

Jesus does not ask for payment for his healings as was the practice for some healers of his time. One finds in some of the midrash of that time that "when Aesculapius has rendered help, he demands a fee which has often been agreed beforehand, a silver pig, a gold statuette, 200 drachmas, or up to 2000 staters."[17] For his work, Jesus desires gratitude, not for himself but for the Father, "in order that the physical benefit may not be unaccompanied by spiritual blessing (Lk 17:17ff.)."[18]

The healings that are reported in the gospel are always closely related to Christ's preaching and teaching. Healing was a part of the message. As those who came with open ears heard the message, so those open to the healing effects of encountering Jesus were healed (Mt 2:24; Mk 3:10; Lk 5:15; 6:18). The healings were not quantitatively significant, they did not remove all the suffering in the world or even in Israel, but their quality gave an indication that no sickness or weakness was too great to be mastered. "The healing activity of Jesus threw a new light on disease and death."[19] The healings demonstrated that no disease was ultimate, no disease was eternal, none could resist the power of God.

Manner of Healing

The healing stories, as they are recorded, though covered with various later additions, give some indication of the manner in which Jesus healed. Jesus was not the only one in his time to heal, as indicated above, but his manner of doing it was somewhat distinguishable. As one writer described it, "the mode of healing practiced by Jesus is infinitely simple, externally unimpressive, but inwardly so much the more powerful. It hardly contains the first beginnings of rational therapy."[20] There are no magic formulas for healings in the gospels. While Jesus at times uses the very common gesture of touching or laying on hands, he never employs magical means or processes, like the majority of the miracle workers outside of the New Testament. "The miracles of Jesus are evoked by the powerful Word of Jesus, which has nothing to do with magic."[21]

The most common means of healing is Jesus' word of power, his command (Mk 1:41; 2:10; Mt 8:9). This method is not sharply distinguishable from the rabbis of his time, but clearly different from the rituals of the non-Jewish healers. St. John's accounts of Jesus' healings emphasize the power of Christ's word to heal. The recovery of the nobleman's son (Jn 4:46ff.) is effected by the mere word of Jesus at a distance. "The saving Word of Jesus either bursts or surmounts all inner barriers and thus brings salvation according to the stories of healing in the gospel."[22]

Jesus' word is described as effecting health, bringing life on all levels of a person, a person who hears it and responds to it.

The word of Jesus, however, usually has power in relation to the person of Jesus. If anything is evident about Jesus' healings, it is that they happen most often through a personal relationship with him. "In the New Testament the compelling force of the personality of the Healer is the decisive matter,"[23] and it is to those who are open to responding to him that health is restored. Walter Grundmann writes that it is "the personal relationship between God and Jesus on the one side and Jesus and men on the other which works the miracle."[24]

I have come to see the intense love of Jesus as the central element in his mission to heal and save, and that awareness has shed new light on my understanding of the healing ministry. The person of Jesus stands at the heart of the healing stories. "In all the varied literature of ancient and modern miracle stories, we do not find anything which remotely approaches, let alone surpasses, the holy and merciful love of Jesus."[25] The uniqueness of his love is evident in its intensity and its comprehensiveness.

It is understandable then, that the evangelists

reserve the word σπλαγχνιζομαι (moved with pity), to describe Jesus' concern for those suffering, since it captures the totality of God's love and everlasting mercy for mankind. Jesus' manifestation of divine love through his person, flows from an intense communication with the Father. It is not surprising, then, to notice that the gospel writers at times explicitly mention the prayer of Jesus in connection with his healing encounters (Mk 7:34; 9:29). We might even allow a possible relationship between Jesus going off to "be by himself with the Father" and the ability he had to effect change and restore health in people's lives.

Faith Relationship

Jesus' manner of healing demanded a response on the part of those asking for health. As was mentioned above, his concern was not to do the fantastic, to perform for his own sake. He gave no satisfactory results to those only seeking wonders. In many of the significant healing accounts, Jesus is described as demanding faith (Mk 5:36; 6:5; 9:23; Mt 8:10), but it is important to try to understand exactly what is meant by faith.

According to Alan Richardson, the contemporary use of the word "faith" in the psychological sense "has little in common with the faith of which the gospel writers are speaking; that is, a saving, personal, believing relationship with Christ."[26] The faith associated with the healing stories includes conviction of the power of God and of Jesus, "but it also is a personal relationship of trust. Trust in the merciful love of God, humble surrender, obedience and self-giving are inseparable from it."[27] (Mt 8:5ff.).

Faith in the gospels is more than intellectual acceptance of ideas. It includes trust, decision, openness to new vision, a receptivity to a deeper encounter with the presence of the divine. The gospels suggest the need for "faith which illuminates the inner meaning of the miracle without which Jesus does not consider it fitting to accomplish the healing."[28] because the effects of Jesus' encounter are never limited to the physical change. Faith engages the entire person and moves toward a continued relationship involving commitment and service.

The faith that is part of the healings of Jesus is distinct from the faith demanded by Aesculapius, a pagan healer contemporary with Jesus.

"Aesculapius demands strict belief in the miracle,"[29] which is not true of Jesus. Jesus is concerned about a relationship that goes deeper than a simple yes to an event. His life portrays a trust relationship with the Father that is focused on more ultimate realities than the success of one happening. Albrecht Oepke writes:

> Under severe temptation he himself maintains his faith even where the miraculous help of God is not displayed (Mt 26:36ff. par., 52ff.). Similarly, he acknowledges particularly the faith which maintains itself victoriously in spite of all opposition (Mt 15:21ff. par. cf. Jn 20:29). Faith is thus a decisive condition of fellowship with God. It receives, not merely healing of the body, but full health or salvation for the whole personality (Mk 5:34 par.; Mk 10:52; Lk 7:50; 17:19).[30]

Effects of Healing

The effects of healing relationships which were part of Christ's life always seem to be described as totally on the physical level. According to Hermann Beyer's evaluation of the healing texts, the described result of the intervention of Jesus is always "that the sick person is fully cured."[31] His healings brought immediate relief from physical suffering, which when it came on the Sabbath caused no small interchange between Jesus and the Jewish leaders.

The healings of Jesus, however, also went beyond the visible. It seems that in the understanding of Jesus, and consequently in the understanding of the evangelist, the person was never "fully healed" until he accepted the miracle of divine salvation. The cleansing of the ten lepers in Luke's gospel (Lk 17:11–19) indicates that only the one who accepted the cleansing miracle in connection with divine salvation was fully made whole. We can conjecture as to what environment Luke is addressing, but, in any case, he seems to be counteracting the false notion that where there is curing, there is salvation. The cures in the New Testament are never separate from the work of salvation. They are only part of bringing people to a more profound wholeness of life.

In the New Testament the overall effect of the miracles is victory in the conflict with forces which struggle for mastery over the world. They are demonstrations of the power of the person of

31

Jesus "by which he makes it plain that with him
the kingdom of God has broken into this suffering world."[32] There is a distinct external witness
value which accompanies the healing encounters
of Christ's ministry. "In face of them the Baptist
ought to see, and even opponents are forced to
recognize, that the royal dominion of God has
come to them (Mt 12:28; Lk 17:21)."[33] Their witness is to the deeper realities and relationships
that are part of the world. The effects of Jesus'
healings are an intricate part of the proclamation
that God cares about his people, that he lives
among his people. "The healing acts of Jesus
were themselves the message that he had come
to set men free."[34]

The healing that Jesus effected grew out of his
concern for people. He suffered when they suf-
fered, and rejoiced when they found wholeness.
Morton Kelsey writes that the healing ministry of
Jesus was "the logical result of the incarnation;
God so loved the world that he gave his only
Son; Jesus so loved that he healed."[35]

Summary

Jesus did not eliminate all suffering. When he
did free someone from physical suffering, how-

ever, he did so in the context of liberating them on a deeper level in order that they might experience the inner freedom of salvation. He gave them a chance to receive a broader perspective of health. Jesus showed a genuine care and concern for people, not to receive money or fame, but to let them experience the healing effects of God's love. He demonstrated the love of the Father in his life situation. He manifested divine love through his personality and that manifestation was the manner of his healing work. To all who did accept him, to all who responded to his prior love with a subsequent trust and openness, he brought health, health on all levels of their person. It was left to the believing community, the church, to continue the healing ministry.

CHAPTER III

Healing Together with Suffering

> The Sanhedrin called in the apostles and had
> them whipped. They ordered them not to speak
> again about the name of Jesus, and afterwards
> dismissed them. The apostles for their part left
> the Sanhedrin full of joy that they had been
> judged worthy of ill-treatment for the sake of the
> Name (Acts 5:40–41).

In carrying on the healing ministry of Jesus,
the early Christians soon came to realize that suffering was also a part of that mission. If they
were going to manifest a risen Christ, the intense
love that he lived, they would have to first accept
the painful surrender of their own desires to the
values that he spoke of and manifested. They
would have to put up with the physical privation
that was part of traveling to make that manifestation known to others, as well as the ridicule, im-

prisonment, and even persecution from those who would rather not be disturbed.

Accounts of early church happenings indicate that the apostles found themselves with healing abilities similar to that of Jesus. Though the healing stories of the apostles, as accounts of Jesus' healings, are intermingled with the faith of the author as well as his purpose for writing, they witness to some manifestations of power and change among those who had a close relationship to Jesus.

The Commission to Heal

There seems to be some question as to exactly how the power to heal was given to the followers of Jesus. "In some sources the power to heal was viewed as bestowed directly on certain people as their vocation—a nontransferable grace or charisma."[36] This view is most evident in Paul's letter to the Corinthians. He speaks of it as an individual gift of grace, "as part of the endowment of the commissioned witness."[37] In other places it was considered "a function of the church as a corporate entity. The individual then mediated the spiritual power of the church."[38]

This understanding finds expression in the letter of James (5:13–20). These different views will find expression throughout Christian history. The reality revealed in either case is that healing power was manifested in the early communities.

Each of the synoptic writers recorded Jesus commissioning his disciples to continue his teaching and healing work. Although one can argue whether the charge in Mark 6:7–13 and its parallel texts has validity for all believers, or just the Twelve, it is certainly clear that the early Christians were aware of a commission to continue the work of Jesus, including preaching and healing. It would seem that such an awareness grew out of Jesus himself, from his preaching and his life example.

The healing power which the members of the early community share is the power of Christ and as such it is the power of God "which they possess only in personal faith."[39] It derives its origin from their association and continued relationship to Jesus himself. As in his case so with the disciples, this power is not for self-glorification or any self-seeking use (Mt 10:8). Such use would be to miss the essential point of the gift (Lk 10:20; Mt 7:22).

Interesting to note, there is "no transmission of power from master to the disciple"[40] as would be the case in the transference of magical power. It is simply in acceptance of the commission and in openness to the power of the Spirit of Jesus that the early church is endowed with the ability to make people whole.

The Power of the Spirit of Jesus

Luke, in the Acts of the Apostles, describes Jesus endowing the disciples with power through his Spirit to proclaim the message (Acts 4:33) and also work miracles (Acts 4:7). It is in personal fellowship with the Spirit of Jesus that the power of Jesus is manifested. The power of his name is only available to those who "know" his name. Walter Grundmann describes it in this way:

> As power and might belong essentially to Christ, the concept of power is linked indissolubly with that of the Spirit. In the Spirit, Christ is present to the apostle as the Dispenser of Power, and in this personal fellowship, granted in and by the πνευμα (Spirit) the apostle is as the Lord. He is not this of himself, but of and by his Lord.[41]

37

St. Paul indicates an awareness that his work of proclaiming and healing is always sustained by his personal union with Christ. Though the New Testament only records healings effected by leaders of communities, it indicates that their ability to do so is derived from their interiorization of the Spirit of Jesus. The communities gathered that each person might develop a "true, lasting, and indissoluble relationship with Christ and attachment to him (cf. Gal 2:20; 4:19),[42] an attachment or relationship that was the basis for effectively changing the lives of people around them. The letter of James (5:13–20) indicates an awareness of the need to unite the infirmed person to the larger community through a representative, which most likely would be the leader or "elder" in a community. His concern manifested the community's concern, his prayer manifested the community's faith relationship with Jesus, his encounter seems to have brought health to the one who was sick (Jas 5:15) and may have been the occasion of a sinner returning (Jas 5:19). That this ability was not just limited to the leaders may be indicated in the first letter to the Corinthians, chapter 12.

If the New Testament gives us any indication

of the early church's experience of healing, it shows healing as being inseparable from the larger mission of preaching salvation. Early writings place healing and preaching together (Mt 9:35f.; 11:4; Lk 9:1–6). Healings were concrete manifestations of the message of salvation. Jesus preached by manifesting through word and deed the unselfish, divine love of his Father which, as indicated in chapter two, brought healing and salvation to those who encountered him with openness. The words he spoke were not separate from the manifestation of an unselfish love and concern through his personality. Together they proclaimed and effected health for the sick and salvation for those seeking deeper wholeness. The early church continued proclaiming the message by manifesting the Spirit of Jesus, the personality of Jesus, in their lives and in their words, which had similar effects.

The Experience of Suffering

Continuing the work of Jesus caused disturbances among the people which angered the public leaders. The early church gradually discovered that its activity caused healing to some but it brought anger and resentment from others. The dynamism of a living relationship with Christ affected change in people's lives, change that threatened religious and political leaders to the point of wanting to eradicate the sources of such change. The Acts of the Apostles indicates the Sanhedrin's discontent with the disturbances caused by members of the early community (Acts 4:1–6; 5:17–40), which led to inflicting punishment on at least some of them. The Acts of the Apostles also describe Paul as suffering from ridicule and beatings by some Jews of Antioch and Iconium (Acts 14:1–7, 19) because of his preaching.

In Acts 16:16–24 he is described as curing a slave girl, which caused him to be flogged and imprisoned. Paul summarized his sufferings involved in preaching the message of Jesus in 2 Corinthians 11:24–28.

The early church must have searched to understand the pain that was part of its mission, to arrive at what it meant to "carry one's cross." It seems that Paul expresses the developing theology of Christian suffering most explicitly.

We notice that his talk concerning suffering is usually with reference to his missionary vocation, the persecution or ridicule that results from the Christian mission (Acts 14:22; 20:23; 2 Cor 11:23-29). At times he refers to the suffering and pain that is part of interiorizing values which Jesus manifested (Gal 5:19-21; Rom 8:13). Often it is difficult to distinguish exactly to which of these he is referring (2 Cor 1:6; Phil 3:10-11; Col 1:24), since both are a part of the mission. In his letter to the Galatians (Gal 4:14), Paul gives indication that he was sick at one time while with them, but in developing a meaningful understanding of suffering he does not mention his sickness or the sickness of others.

It seems that the early church sought most to find meaning in the suffering that was part of being a follower of Christ. One explanation was that suffering was a necessary part of discipleship. This idea is often expressed in Paul's writings. According to him, "the apostolate involves both a work to be done and suffering to be borne if the body of Christ is to be built up and the life of Christ to be diffused to new members."[43] Paul also expressed a feeling that his suffering (perhaps implying any Christian's suffering) benefited the whole body of Christ through encouragement (2 Cor 1:4-7).

It seems that, with time, suffering as part of

the mission came to be a sign of salvation (Phil 1:28). Those who endured it "with joy" became witnesses to the deeper realities of life. Its value was derived from the message that it proclaimed.

In Philippians 1:29, Paul explains suffering for Christ as a "special privilege." It is seen as a special grace to proclaim the message, or it can provide a person with a more effective means of alleviating the pains of others, an idea implied in Paul's discussion of his own suffering. He is aware that the words that come from one who suffers can have added strength deriving from the person's acceptance of his situation.

The second letter to the Corinthians expresses another value that Paul finds in personal suffering, that is, it allows God's power to be made manifest (2 Cor 12:6–10; 2 Cor 13:4). If any text might refer to suffering from disease it is 2 Cor 12:6–10 where Paul speaks of his "thorn in the flesh." The value of the suffering is seen in that it "forced" him to humility and surrender before the Creator.

Paul's most predominant teaching concerning suffering of Christians, which probably reflects the early church's teaching, is that we as Christians must manifest the disposition of Christ in meeting the trials of life (Rom 15:2-3; Phil 2:5-8; 1 Tim 6:13). This we do by identifying our suffering with that of Christ, by recognizing that it is not just a means to an end, but a way of life along with the person of Christ. It establishes a relationship, making us aware of the love manifested in Christ's total surrender. Joy is possible in suffering, not because pain is good, but because it is endured in union with Christ. The relationship is the source of joy. The value lies in the relationship, not in the suffering. Joseph Blenkinsopp expresses it as follows:

> Out of the baptismal faith-relationship of the community with Christ a new and deeper level of communication is created. This implies also a "koinona" in suffering which both links together the sufferings of the individual Christians with those of Christ and binds the sufferings of the whole body together (cf. 2 Cor 1:5-7).[44]

Suffering in the thought of Paul then becomes a way of knowing Jesus more fully through fellowship in his suffering: "... that I may know him and the power of his resurrection, and may share his suffering, becoming like him in his death, that if possible I may attain to the resurrection from the dead" (Phil 3:10–11). This "fellowship in suffering" refers to the suffering that was part of the mission, the inner struggle to surrender to a life manifesting Christ's values and the external punishment that resulted from such a life of proclamation. This realization might explain why "St. Paul, who makes such a point of telling people to imitate him as he imitates Christ, and who adds that his desire is to share his sufferings by reproducing the pattern of his death (Phil 3:10) sees no contradiction in healing sickness."[45]

It is difficult to systematize the thoughts of Paul on suffering but however we evaluate his writings and his life as described in the New Testament, there is evidence that he respected healing where healing was possible (1 Cor 12:9), while at the same time he found value in suffering that was inescapable. The type of suffering that he most frequently speaks of as potentially being redemptive is the suffering inherent in preaching the kingdom, yet when his prayer concerning "the thorn in the flesh" (2 Cor 12:8–10) did not bring about his desired effect, he found value for himself in that suffering as well.

If the writings of Luke and Paul are an indication of early church happenings and understandings then it is evident that the healing work of Christ continued after his resurrection and that it met with reactions very much like those he encountered.

New Testament Summary

The New Testament leaves us aware that Christ through his person changed people's lives and made them whole. His manifestations of concern and unselfish love brought health to the diseased along with a deeper wholeness to all who approached him with openness. The apostles and early disciples were examples of some who were made whole by their encounter with his person, and having been strengthened in wholeness by the power of his resurrected Spirit, they went about continuing his work.

The texts of the gospels leave evidence that Christ suffered in "making his dwelling among us" and he suffered at the hands of those who detested the disturbances caused by his love. Other New Testament writings indicate that his followers experienced similar sufferings. Such

45

suffering came to be understood as part of the mission, valuable in that it proclaims a relationship. It is an occasion for manifesting unselfish love. The suffering that derives from sickness or the indwelling of evil, however, is generally only spoken of as being healed. In 2 Corinthians 12, Paul hints at some personal weakness in which he finds value for himself, the value of remaining humble before God, that his power might be manifest. The value is in the manifestation.

The near silence in the New Testament concerning the value of suffering that derives from sickness or the indwelling of evil, and the realization that healing was part of the message, left the church with the continual challenge of searching for a viable position between healing and suffering that would adequately respond to the diseases and forces of evil which would be a part of their lives.

CHAPTER IV

Historical Development
of Healing and Suffering

> Since in God's wisdom the world did not come
> to know him through "wisdom," it pleased God
> to save those who believe through the absurdity
> of the preaching of the gospel (1 Cor 1:21).

While growing Christian communities faced
the rejection and even outright persecution from
outsiders, they probably wrestled at least as
strenuously among themselves with the question
of the value and purpose of suffering from disease and the indwelling of evil, and their ability
to deal with it. Different historical happenings
and various philosophical ideas would influence
the church's understanding of healing, causing
the development of practices that hardly resem-
ble the healing encounters spoken of in the last
two chapters. In this section I will try to highlight
what seem to be some significant happenings in

the development of the church's healing mission. This sketch is by no means comprehensive—I feel it is, however, in keeping with the facts of history.

The Apologists

The scanty records remaining from the second and third centuries give us indications that healing was evident after the apostles had died. A number of the apologists make references to Christian healings taking place. Morton Kelsey cites these examples:

> Quadratus, one of the earliest apologists wrote in Rome that the works of the Savior had continued to his time and that the continued presence of men who had been healed left no question as to the reality of physical healing. Justin Martyr tells in several places how Christians healed in the name of Jesus Christ.[46]

We find in the writings of Irenaus references to healings. "Irenaus attested to almost the same range of healings as we have found in the Gospels and Acts. All kinds of bodily infirmities as well as many different diseases had been

48

cured."[47] It seems necessary to understand these reports with the realization that it was a practice in the hellenistic world to attribute healing powers to significant religious personages. In that light we could conceive of pagans attributing cures to some prominent people. The faith of the apologists led them to see the work of God in the cures that happened in relation to people who believed in him. Origen reports that the gift of healing extended even to Greeks and barbarians who came to believe in Jesus and they at times effected "amazing cures" by his name. In *Against Celsus* Origen writes the following:

> Some give evidence of their having received through this faith a marvelous power by the cures which they perform, invoking no other name over those who need their help than that of the God of all things, and of Jesus, along with a mention of His history. For by these means we too have seen many persons freed from grievous calamities, and from distractions of mind and madness, and countless other ills.[48]

It seems intriguing that Irenaus mentions that "no fee was charged for healing performed by Christians, a practice quite different from the pagan temples of healing such as the famous ones in Epidaurus and Pergamum."[49] It is difficult to decipher the extent of that practice or to translate exactly what it says, but it may at least hint at a non-self-seeking motive for Christian healing.

While the apologists give evidence of the continuation of healing after New Testament times, they begin seeing the healings separate from a relationship to Jesus and the deeper realities that he was proclaiming by them. The apologists took on the needed task of defending the legitimacy and authenticity of the Christian religion and in their writings healing stories were used to prove the divine origin of the Christian religion. The stories were separated from their context. The apologists used the stories to emphasize the effects of God among his people, but gave no indication as to what caused these effects except that they must be of divine origin. This separation would leave people to search for exactly what it was that made such fantastic things happen. It may have contributed to an understanding of healings as purely God's work, breaking natural law where he wished, rather than seeing God's power active in the world through the decisions of Christians to let his power be manifest through their personalities, their relationships. Neither understanding denies God's power to heal, but the apologists' emphasis seemed to locate that power so distantly, so much God's alone, that Christians would hardly have expected their manifestation of a deep love for another, the God-likeness in them, to be of any healing value. As the church used more and more structures and rituals to occasion healings, the power of encountering someone with love, as Jesus did, received less emphasis.

Martyrdom

Records of the second and third centuries also give evidence of persecutions of Christians and believers who were willing to die for their faith. Morton Kelsey sees an interconnection between the healing ministry of the early Christians and the courage to accept martyrdom. He writes this:

For nearly three centuries this healing, centrally experienced, was an indispensable ingredient of Christian life. The same strengthening force was at work, not only in dealing with physical and mental

51

disease but in meeting persecution. The power, the same profound experience, was given to these men and women to meet agonizing death, often by slow degree, without yielding to save themselves by repudiating Christianity. Thus the martyrs, too, stood as continuous evidence of a power able to strengthen them beyond normal expectations of human life, and of the Christian's relation to the source of power.[50]

The early healings as well as the accounts of martyrdom do manifest an intense personal relationship with Christ from which people drew strength to lay down their lives or to affect change in the lives of people around them.

It seems that after Christianity became an accepted religion in the fourth century, there was less need to manifest the "strength beyond normal expectation" that was part of a close relationship to Christ. Martyrdom had been viewed as the "ideal instance of union with Christ in trial." After the persecutions, the question arose as to whether or not there was some substitute for martyrdom as a way of uniting oneself to Christ. Some saw celibacy as a substitute renunciation. Others responded to the world's becoming "friendly to Christianity" by returning to the desert "to find once more the detachment, austerity, and fervor they had known but could no longer know in a life suddenly become too easy."[51] It is in the desert that people began to see a merit in inflicting suffering upon themselves. Though their practice originally stems from the nobleness that they saw in martyrdom, they gradually come to see a good in suffering itself, rather than seeing the value in the relationship to Jesus which such a lifestyle was meant to enhance or manifest.

Influence of Philosophy

This development is related to the dualistic influences that met the early church as it expanded. These influences were expressed in Gnostic and Manichean ideas which downgraded the value of the body. We find records of the desert fathers beating their bodies to bring them under submission for the benefit of their soul. "Under the influence of the Desert Fathers, severe asceticism was held up as the model of Christian perfection; man's body is to be distrusted and not just tamed; it is to be put to

death through various mortifications and penances."[52] Though the early church saw value in
integrating the values of Jesus into their lives,
this newer view of man made physical healing
undesirable to the "ideal" of Christianity. This
dichotomy of body and soul seems to have had a
long-range effect on the healing mission of the
church.

John Cassian (360-ca.432), who set forth much
of the thought behind Western monasticism,
presents an understanding of healing that origi-
nates with the Desert Fathers. His understanding
of healing and suffering became a great influence
on all of Western spirituality since his works
were the first summary of spiritual theology in
the West. In speaking of the healing gifts among
the Desert Fathers, he notes that they "would
never use them unless perhaps extreme and unavoidable necessity drove them to do so."[53] He
sees the need to warn the church about the
danger of using the gift of healing, lest one "lose
his very soul by too much attention to healing
men's bodies."[54]

Pope Gregory the Great (540–604), a notable
doctor of the Western church, picked up this
understanding of healing and the suffering from
sickness and developed it further in his much

respected *Book of Pastoral Rule*. He saw bodily illnesses as one more way in which God chastised his children. It was seen as "a mark of God's correction, sometimes inflicted by the negative powers with his approval to bring moral renewal."[55] His thought left not so much a question of the possibility of physical healing through the Spirit, but of the advisability of such action. In his *Dialogues* he writes that "the intercession of holy people is powerful with God even to the working of miracles,"[56] but his strong idea that illness is a scourge from God for the purpose of one's moral reform made it dangerous and non-desirable to expect physical healing.

By the seventh century the understanding of sickness had moved to one of the Old Testament notions that sickness was the result of God's wrath at the sins of men. Bodily sickness or suffering was viewed as a good for the soul. "Curing the body without curing the soul was valueless, if not dangerous. Any kind of healing began to be treated with suspicion...."[57]

Sacrament of Anointing

The influence of such views of the human person and of suffering seems to be evident in the

55

development of the sacrament of the anointing of the sick. Before the eighth century there was no official rite of anointing as exists today, but a close examination of some of the oldest consecratory prayers prayed for the sick by individuals who got oil from the bishop shows that "the numerous formulas which verbally deal with bodily health are expressing in fact a deeper intention that is concerned with the healing of man in his entirety."[58] They express an expectation of total health through the anointing and prayer of faith.

This expectation for the anointing to bring health dwindled as bodily punishment or suffering grew to be seen as valuable for the soul. The therapeutic value of bodily suffering was also evident in the development of tariff penance at this time, which placed a high value on doing physical penance for one's sins. This practice of penance grew out of the Irish monasteries where severe bodily austerity was a marked feature. As penance became closely associated with the anointing of the sick, people would wait "until death was inevitable" for anointing so they could "minimize for themselves as much as possible the rigorous penitential requirements,"[59] that were part of confessing their sins. This rite of extreme unction was quite different from the healing encounters evident in the New Testament. The healing effect of anointing was never denied, but the sacrament came to be administered principally for the purpose of gaining some spiritual advantage. "The chance that healing might happen could not be entirely denied, but there was no expectation that the spiritual could affect the physical body."[60]

The power of Christ to heal was not expected to be manifested in extreme unction or in penance. The intellectuals of the Middle Ages sought to explain that nonexpectancy by theological arguments when in many ways the philosophical assumptions caused most of the unanswered questions. Church thought and teaching went from wondering if it was advisable to ask for physical healing lest the person not be brought to moral betterment (the purpose for which the sickness was assumed to be "sent"), to the question as to whether God could really break into this world in any such visible way, assuming that revelation was completed after Christ ascended.

The reformers of the sixteenth century questioned the spiritual value of physical penances or various practices that evolved from them (indulgences and payment for spiritual benefit), but they never effectively investigated the philosophical influences that had reidentified what it meant to "take up one's cross." They questioned the effectiveness of the sacramental actions of penance and extreme unction but offered no more effective occasions for restoring people to health. Their questioning brought some reforms, but in regard to the healing practice of the church it made little difference. Their questioning drew a defensive response from the official Catholic teaching. The Council of Trent redefined the specific requirements for the sacrament of extreme unction, including the specification that it was only for those in danger of death. The official healing ministry of the church remained at that level until recent times.

The official church teaching and practice reflects a development away from healing encounters, but the records leave us indications that the Christian message was never completely without healing experiences. Allowing for embellishments and exaggerations, it seems evident that some significant healings took place in certain communities and in relationships with certain believers, some of whom have been called saints. To study the stories of healing in order to evaluate exactly what occurred would leave us aware of the exaggerations, but it would also indicate that healing encounters have been happening throughout the complex mixture of influences and decisions as the church continued to develop.

Summary

The history of Christianity in the West indicates various developments in the understanding of healing and of suffering. Healing became separated from an emphasis on relationships and encounters, resulting in part from the need to defend the Christian religion from verbal attack and perhaps in part from the more organized structures that were necessary to accomodate the many newcomers to the faith after Christianity was officially recognized in the fourth century. Through the influence of philosophy and a distortion of the idea of martyrdom, bodily suffering became separated from a relationship to Christ and came to be thought of as "sent for one's moral good," and it was questionable whether one should pray for healing. Eventually God's power to heal was not expected to be manifested and theologians found reasons to explain that nonexpectancy. In light of these historical developments, and keeping in mind the works and example of Jesus regarding suffering and healing, we can search for a viable Christian understanding of the experience of suffering and healing.

CHAPTER V

Suffering and Acceptance

> He advanced a little and fell to the ground, pray-
> ing that if it were possible this hour might pass
> him by. He kept saying, "Abba (O Father), you
> have the power to do all things. Take this cup
> away from me. But let it be as you would have it,
> not as I" (Mk 14:35–36).

In searching for value in the human experience
of suffering, it is helpful to distinguish different
types of suffering and various responses to them
as found in Christian history. It seems necessary
to distinguish between the suffering that we in
some way choose, the type of suffering that
stems from our goal in life (i.e., the ache of bodily
training for a sport or the discomfort of living
simply), from the unavoidable suffering in life
(i.e., the suffering that results from birth defects,
accidents, or illnesses).

SUFFERING AND ACCEPTANCE

Knowing how Jesus responded to the sufferings that were part of his mission has often been a source of comfort to Christians as they faced the hardships of a given life style. As I researched chapter one, dealing with the pains in Jesus' life, I found his responses to be a comfort to me. But the questions that lie at the roots of this study[61] center on this latter type of unavoidable suffering in life, and more specifically on the suffering stemming from unavoidable illness or disease. In talking about a response to this type of suffering we can take some ideas from Jesus' response to his pains, but we must also remember that Jesus often healed the suffering of others.

The gospels and other New Testament writings say very little about suffering from illness or disease, except for the healing stories, where the person's encounter with Jesus, or a follower of Jesus, brings health. There are no words of Jesus that encourage a person to bear such suffering. His references to suffering are all concerned with the suffering stemming from his mission. The writings of Paul as well, when speaking of suffering, focus almost exclusively on sufferings deriving from his goal in life.

SUFFERING AND ACCEPTANCE

The fact that Jesus responded somewhat differently to suffering deriving from his goal in life than to suffering stemming from illness has caused the church to struggle continually in search of an understanding of healing in the light of redemptive suffering. Records of the church's history indicate that certain explanations of the value of suffering stemming from illnesses were heavily colored by outside influences to the point of putting them at odds with the Christian message of healing. They would not pray for healing because they believed that suffering was valuable. Suffering became so "redemptive" that healing hardly had value.

In what way can suffering be given value without detracting from the message of healing which is central to the gospel?

An understanding of suffering stemming from illness has to deal with trying to search out some possible values that can be a part of that human experience. We as humans do not like pain, but the reality of the matter is that it exists. Our mind struggles to answer why. The Christian searches to find what Jesus might have said, how he might have found meaning in the pain of life. Even though his references are not to the suffering that comes from illness, his disposition and the value he places on the suffering of his life may give some insight into possible values for the unavoidable suffering from illness or disease.

Suffering Chosen For a Goal

The value that Jesus found in his suffering does not stem from the suffering itself, but from the value of the relationship that it proclaimed and the new relationship that it made possible between God and his people. In regard to this suffering, his life spoke of acceptance, acceptance of the pain that was part of restoring a broken relationship between God and mankind.

It seems clear that he did not enjoy pain any more than other human beings and that at times he would have liked to be freed from it: "Abba, you have the power to do all things. Take this cup away from me. But let it be as you would have it, not as I" (Mk 14:36). He desires to be free of pain, yet if it is part of a larger plan, part of his relationship to the Father, he will accept it. The cross remains a symbol of a disposition of surrender to the Father and acceptance of the realities that were part of his mission.

SUFFERING AND ACCEPTANCE

History indicates how the early church struggled to comprehend the paradox of a suffering and crucified messiah. It was not supposed to happen through pain and suffering, but it did, "a stumbling block to the Jews and an absurdity to Gentiles," but to the believer, the power of God. "The 'religion of the cross' if faith on this basis can ever be so called, does not elevate and edify in the usual sense, but scandalizes... but by this scandal, it brings liberation into the world."[62] The incarnation of Jesus, his "emptying himself" and acceptance of the sufferings that were part of his mission, manifested an unselfish love, an intense relationship to the Father that was almost too profound for the world to comprehend.

The surrender of his will to the Father's manifested a love so intense that it empowers his followers to accept suffering as well. They accepted the external pain of rejection and persecution as well as the internal pains of transforming their desires into the values that Jesus lived and proclaimed. The acceptance of these pains manifested a love relationship to Jesus, proclaiming that their source of life and salvation was in him. Karl Rahner expresses this value as follows:

SUFFERING AND ACCEPTANCE

Active renunciation of one's own happiness as is contained in surrender to pain and sorrow is still the clearest practical confession of the fact that man, conscious of his powerlessness in the face of the God of forgiveness and elevating grace, expects his salvation from above and not from himself and hence can and will sacrifice his ego and its values, those values which are powerless to procure his salvation.[63]

Such a surrender proclaims a deeper reality to life.

We perceive in the life of Jesus a certain acceptance of all that is part of his emptying himself. That acceptance has meaning in that it flows from a relationship to the Father, and insofar as it flows from a relationship, it manifests love, a love that was manifested in his continued free acceptance of all that was part of the redeeming process including death on a cross.

It is up to the followers of Christ to manifest the same loving relationship by accepting the pain that goes with interiorizing his values as well as facing the rejection and hardships that his message brings. It is "man's privilege to share by his sufferings, in the redemptive work of

God."[64] Such suffering is valuable; it is redemptive in that it makes effectual in the present the victory of salvation which Jesus gained (cf. Col 1:24). The total surrender to that mission proclaims a risen Christ.

Suffering from Illness

The Christian response to unavoidable suffering stemming from illness seems to be somewhat different. To directly apply Christ's response to suffering from his life goal to the suffering that stems from physical sickness is to reject the healing ministry of Jesus. Such an application neglects the fact that his response, as reported in the gospels, to the latter type of suffering, was occasionally to heal it. To say that bodily suffering is for the good of the soul is to accept a view of man that would have been foreign to Jesus, that denies the interrelatedness of the whole person, and hardly reflects a recognition of the fact that Jesus healed the whole of the person who accepted his healing presence.

At the same time, to deny the fact that we as Christians are capable of putting value into unavoidable suffering would be to give little credence to the free will of the human person, and little power to the experience of Christ in our lives. Somewhere within these considerations we must respond to suffering in such a way as to proclaim acceptance with an openness to the healing effects of Christ's love.

The response that people make to suffering is often related to the source from which they think it comes. The "problem" of the origin of sickness, then, deserves a few words. For a long time, people have struggled with this question as to the cause of sickness. Generally in the Old Testament it is assumed that sickness among the people came from their disloyalty to the covenant with God. Eventually, among some groups, sickness became identified with a specific sin and certain emotional behaviors became identified with the indwelling of evil. The New Testament gives no "solution" to the "problem" of the origin of sickness, though it indicates some relationships to sin. Later some illnesses came to be recognized as the result of the natural inter-relatedness of nature. More recently scientific research has shown the interrelatedness of emotions such as fear, guilt, or tension with bodily sickness and suffering. In certain cases the human mind simply cannot understand what might be the source of illnesses which cause suffering.

Though the cause of illness and its subsequent suffering may affect our response to it, the value of the response does not derive from the source of the sickness. Jesus' response to the suffering of others may be connected to his understanding of sickness, but the value of his response stems from the love that initiated it, the love that caused him to "dwell among men" that they might have fuller life. The value of the response can exist whether the sickness came from natural interrelatedness or from sin. The redemptive value is not in the suffering itself. John Hick writes the following:

> The contribution which sin and its attendant suffering make to God's plan does not consist in any value intinsic to themselves, but, on the contrary, in the activities whereby they are overcome, namely, redemption from sin, and men's mutual service amid suffering.[65]

Jesus came to redeem sin, to restore relationships, to alleviate fears and meaninglessness in life. He never attempted to eradicate the natural "evils" that are part of life; what he offered was "the conquest of sin, and in that victory the eradication of the fears and the meaninglessness of natural evil."[66] Jesus' response to the sickness that he encountered may reflect more his response to sin than his response to suffering in itself. Since, at times, he saw some interrelatedness between sickness and sin, and since his encounters brought resoration to the person as a whole, it is difficult to know exactly to which he was most directly responding.

Because of the free ability to decide or respond to suffering, it may be an expression of love. If God is love and love involves a cost, then perhaps suffering "is the cost to God of attaining his will through man's free will."[67] By entering time and finitude and accepting pain (Phil 2:5–11), Jesus rejected the notion of equating perfection with security and invulnerability, and through his victory over sin and the fears of death, men came to realize "that the perfection of God is not denied by God's suffering love but is especially evident there."[68] The vulnerability to suffering which is involved in loving is not "ultimately evil," nor intinsically good, but valued in relation to what is expressed in response to it.

70

SUFFERING AND ACCEPTANCE

An Occasion for Spiritual Growth

Suffering from illness for us as Christians has value in that we relate it to our relationship with Jesus. Its value comes from the way in which we allow it to affect our relationship to the person of Christ and the meaning which he found in this life. It is an occasion that demands a response, an occasion that can be valuable for the one suffering as well as for those present to him.

The suffering from sickness in the gospels is always reported as an opportunity for new health, for deeper wholeness flowing from the manifestation of the healing love of Jesus. More will be said of this response in the next chapter, but at least that awareness might cause a person who is suffering to examine some of his dispositions in regard to his total health. It may be the occasion to recognize some deeper, more significant realities in life. It may be a temptation to deliberately cultivate the tolerable pain to avoid a real commitment or decision to be made. It may be an occasion to recognize the giftedness of life and health, to count the days of gifted health rather than the days of sickness. These possible values of suffering become values through a person's decision to make them so. We might recall that the recordings of Jesus' response to the suffering of others often related the occasion to a deeper growth experience (Mk 2:1–12 and par.; Mk 10:52; Lk 17:11–19).

The inescapable suffering stemming from illness may threaten our basic sense of meaning in life, especially if that meaning and security is based on possessions. It is in that sense that suffering is sometimes experienced as an "evil," but such a threat may be the occasion to grow to a deeper realization of the purpose of creation, and our own life in that creation. If we believe that "man is enacting his death . . . through the deeds of his life,"[69] then acceptance of suffering is part of our acceptance of the reality of humanness and one of the steps in accepting death. It can be part of "a life-long practice for that readiness for death,"[70] the type of death that proclaims resurrection.

Dorothee Soelle writes this:

Every acceptance of suffering is an acceptance of that which exists. The denial of every form of suffering can result in a flight from reality in which contact with reality becomes ever thinner, ever more fragmented. It is impossible to remove oneself totally from suffering, unless one removes oneself from life itself, no longer enters into relationships, makes oneself invulnerable.[71]

If indeed death is an active consummation worked out through the life of a person, then acceptance of the reality of life and suffering are preparations for a meaningful death. In the same manner, the choosing of voluntary sufferings or the reflection on the acceptance of suffering as manifested in others or in the person of Christ, can be preparation for a more valuable response to the inescapable sufferings of life.

An Occasion for Redemptiveness

In certain cases the suffering from illness can become an occasion for being of special help to others who are in a similar position of suffering. This redemptive value of suffering is exemplified among the "Christian Fraternity of the Sick," a group of handicapped people who, because of their experience of Jesus amid their suffering, minister to others who are handicapped. "When a person experiences suffering and reflects deeply on the meaning of it in his own life, and in the world, he becomes aware of new depths and creativity in himself."[72] Patricia Lowery, M.M., describes such a person in this way:

> The cries of sufferers find an echo in his heart, and, as they enter more deeply into his life, he will reach out of his weakness to respond with concern, responsibility, and love. As he grows in compassion, so will he grow in greatness of heart. ...Having been "brought low" he stands humble before the other and the silent testimony he presents can be a visible sign of hope to one who is still struggling to find his way on an unknown path.[73]

It is such ministry from weakness that was found to be valuable to the apostle Paul.

Through our relationship to the person of Jesus, the suffering from illness, especially some long-term illnesses, can be transformed into means of bringing health and/or faith to others. The power of such transformed suffering lies in the fact that it manifests both a profound trust relationship with God and a compassionate concern for fellow sufferers. It sharpens our ability to feel with the pains of another. It speaks of surrender, of acceptance of the reality of what is unchangeable in life, and then from that new vantage point, begins changing what is changeable through manifesting the unselfish love of Jesus to other sufferers. It is a way of making Jesus' victory of salvation effectual in the present, "of filling up what is lacking in the sufferings of Christ for the sake of his body, the church" (Col 1:24). "Suffering which so easily retires within itself, when transfigured, can become a sacrament of charity, an effective sign of opening out of one's self to others."[74] Such a witness of accepted suffering professes more profoundly than any words a belief in the transforming power of the love of Christ.

Summary

This understanding of the suffering that touches people's lives through sickness does not remove the hurt of pain. Pain still hurts. Suffering is still unpleasant, but for the person who is seeking to grow in Christ, it can be an occasion to come to a new wholeness or to manifest an acceptance that proclaims a love relationship to others. The value of the occasion of sickness, if it will exist, is placed on it by the person or friends of the person who accept it, who surrender with openness to reality and to the wider possibilities of God's plan. The redemptiveness is in the acceptance, not an apathetic acceptance, but an acceptance that is open to the manifestation of the love of Christ changing what can be changed; an acceptance in expectancy of new wholeness, a type of wholeness that was effected by Jesus and his followers who radiated God's presence through their personalities. It is this attitude of open acceptance of what is that becomes the first step, the necessary faith relationship, to being brought to complete wholeness through an experience of Christ's love made manifest.

CHAPTER VI

The Ministry of Healing Today

> This prayer uttered in faith will reclaim the one who is ill, and the Lord will restore him to health. If he has committed any sins, forgiveness will be his. Hence, declare your sins to one another, and pray for one another, that you may find healing (James 5:15–16).

While the acceptance of suffering has value and is indeed part of the healing process, we need not stop at that beginning stage. If openness to deeper growth through Christ is part of that acceptance, then the value that suffering may have can be viewed as part of the value of being made whole in Christ, or bringing someone else to health.

The world does not exist free from suffering, nor did Jesus heal all illnesses, whether physical, mental, or spiritual, so we must continue to search for meaning and value in suffering, but that value may not cloud the message of healing which is inseparable from the gospel. Central to the gospel message is Jesus' desire to bring the people he met to spiritual health, to a meaningful existence, to harmony with the Father. The writings about Jesus describe his attempts to help people experience and understand the love of the Father and the healing effects which that love could produce in all areas of a person's life. The gospel narratives and other New Testament writings give evidence of certain healing power flowing from God's loving presence made manifest in the lives of people who encountered him. This chapter will reflect what some current ministers of healing find to be important in proclaiming the healing message of the gospel. The basis of their considerations stems from reflection upon healings which they have seen happen through prayerful encounters with other people.

The healing that is possible through an experience of the love of God made manifest ranges in intensity from the healing that occurs in a greeting of peace to the healing of a deep-rooted memory or the mending of a physical wound. This chapter will focus on the more intense healing encounters that cause noticeable long-term changes in a person. Such healings need not be viewed as completely different from the new health we experience in a sincere exchange of Christ's peace, except that the intensity of that peace, that presence, is greater and in that way may have a greater effect.

Interrelatedness Within a Person

Before considering some significant factors in that healing process, it seems necessary to recognize the interrelatedness within a person's makeup. While people experience injury or sickness on one level of their person, either physical, emotional, or spiritual, the source of the sickness may frequently be located on a different level. Within the last hundred years this interrelatedness has been made more conscious through study of the human person.

The effects of emotions upon the physical body have become more clearly detectable in recent times. In speaking about physical diseases, Charles Mayo, M.D., estimates that "the spiritual and psychological factor in disease varies from 65 percent to 75 percent."[75] A recent arti-

79

cle in *Psychology Today*[76] reports that 50 to 80 percent of all diseases have origins in emotional stress. According to the article our body starts late in adolescence to accumulate the effects of stress that will surface as physical disorders when we reach the forties or fifties. The effects of the emotional and physical levels of a person on each other is a constant process, and often it is unconscious. Morton Kelsey writes the following:

> Unconscious fear and anger can react incessantly on a man's heart and kidneys, his stomach, or his entire circulatory system without his knowing it, until the structure of one organ or another has been changed enough to cause him pain.[77]

The emotions that we may instinctively try to repress find their way to the surface in some form.

It is also evident that a person's spiritual level can have effects on the emotions and on the body. Peter Ford writes this concerning his work with mentally disturbed people:

> What I did discover was that many of the patients who suffered from vague somatic and emotional

symptoms were not mentally ill at all, at least not in the usual academic or diagnostic sense. Most of these people were spiritually ill, that is, they were suffering from the result of rejection and prolonged periods of love-deprivation. It was not only human love that they were lacking; they were separated from the love of God.[78]

Ford goes on to say that nearly all disease and ailments that affect the human being affect all three levels of the person.

This interaction among the various aspects of a person is also evident in a more positive sense in the healing ministry. Father Michael Scanlan writes that "many physical diseases disappear after a person has received an inner healing."[79] [By inner healing is meant the healing of the intellectual, volitional, and affective areas (mind, will, and heart) including areas related to the emotions, such as psyche, soul, and spirit.] Barbara Shlemon describes her experience of praying with a woman suffering with a bladder infection:

I felt led to inquire about her past which she graphically described as being in hell. Her husband had deserted the family for another woman leaving

81

her the sole support of three young children. The bitterness in her voice as she related the story told me much more than the words ever could.

We talked about the lack of love being an obstacle to healing and I asked if she were willing to make an act of forgiveness toward her husband. At first she was very defensive, using many arguments to substantiate her right to hate this man who had caused them so much misery. As we talked she gradually came to realize that the hatred was hurting her more than it was punishing him. I asked her to pray a blessing for her husband, forgiving him for neglecting her and the children. Then we prayed the prayer of faith, asking Jesus to touch her body and heal it.[80]

Mrs. Shlemon reports that several weeks later she received a letter telling her that not only had the physical illness disappeared, but that the lady had experienced a "new feeling of joy" in her life.

In the past, as was evident in some understandings of "redemptive suffering" that developed, it was believed that the relationship between levels of the person was limited and one-directional, namely, that the suffering of the physical body could effect the moral status of the soul. At times people seemed certain that the physical sickness of a person "had to be sent by God" for the betterment of his soul. Though a broader understanding of the total interrelatedness of the different levels of a person does not answer the why of suffering, it makes us aware of more possible explanations for the occurrence of a physical malady and gives evidence that healing needs to be directed to the whole person.

The Healing Trinity

The interrelatedness within a person may lead us to recognize the close interrelation between all forms of healing. The physician, the psychotherapist, and the spiritual minister form a "healing trinity," a team that together prepares the conditions for healing to occur. Morton Kelsey writes the following:

Healing occurs when the conditions are right. There are physical conditions which only the physician is qualified to know and prepare. There are also emotional conditions which can be made ready by those trained in psychotherapy. And finally, healing requires conditions of a spiritual nature which can best be seen and helped along by those trained and practiced in the unique traditions of the vital Christian church. Together they make a team of which God has need.[81]

It is important that each member of this healing team recognize, with respect for the other members, his or her ability to affect a person at all levels of their experience. Peter Ford, in focusing primarily on the psychological and spiritual aspects of the healing process, points out how the lack of recognition of the competence of psychology, or the lack of recognition of the power of the gospel, can impede healing.

Some people reduce the ability to effect an inner healing to the accepting relationship and the psychological skills that a therapist offers a patient. While it is evident from the gospel texts and from experience that God works through nature, through the relationships of people, his power is not limited to just the natural occasion. When the therapist must wait, the believer can pray; where the therapist shows concern, the believer can show love that manifests a greater, more powerful, unrelenting love of God. While both of these can "sweep away repressing and inhibiting complexes, and liberate the forces lying latent in the soul of the patient, restoring him to life and health,"[82] each must be recognized for its own value. The healing effects of the experience of the love of God need to be recognized and understood as a part of that team.

There has been a tendency to reduce the effects of each member of the "healing trinity" to his particular area (e.g., the doctor affects only the body, the spiritual minister affects only the soul). One consequence of that tendency is to view healing through spiritual means as distinct from nature and possibly contrary to natural law. A look at the New Testament and the healings of Jesus indicates that it is within the very naturalness of relationships that Jesus healed. It is the natural event of an encounter with another person that he transformed into a healing encounter through the intensity with which his personality manifested the unselfish love of God. His encounter accelerated, made possible, or transcended the natural healing process in the same way that people or prayer teams today do through prayer and manifestation of God's presence, though perhaps not with the same intensity. This is not to say that God's power is limited to the natural occurrences, but rather that within those occurrences his power is revealed.

Significant Factors in Healing

This understanding of person, with complexities and interrelatedness, still leaves us uncertain as to exactly how to pray with someone who is sick, or exactly what areas of suffering will be affected. To shed some light on these uncertainties, we might consider what seem to be some significant factors in the spiritual healing ministry, factors which in part apply to the other areas of healing as well.

1) An initial factor in the healing process is to examine the question, "Do you really want to be healed?" Barbara Shlemon points out that the Lord will not violate the gift of the free will. We must desire to be healed. Sometimes this may involve possible unconscious resistance to healing, such as a deep-rooted reward for not being whole, or the fear of an honest look at oneself. Such resistance, whether conscious or unconscious, can hardly be thought to result in redemptive suffering. Michael Scanlan writes that "many come for inner healing but are unwilling to forgive an injury or forget a resentment. They

wish to have peace and still nurture the wrongs against them."[83] We must decide for a healing with an acceptance of the new responsibilities of health.

2) One factor in healing that seems to get more attention than others, and at times unsound attention, is the element of a faith relationship which is part of the healing process. The statement "if you have faith, you will be healed," can be as true as it can be false. Faith is *one* of the significant factors in a healing encounter. Though faith is essential, it may be located in the sick person, or in the one or many occasioning the healing, or in both. Wherever it is located, it is a faith relationship, a belief that is not just intellectual but experiential as well and manifested as such. The faith that is part of the healing process is a faith that engages the entire person, a trust relationship that flows from "being grasped by the Ultimate Reality, which is God."[84] It is distinct from the trust in our own ability; it is a trust relationship with God, a confidence in his faithfulness, his power and his goodness, assuring us that "whatever is ultimately the most loving thing will happen in response to my prayer for healing."[85]

While in the gospels at times faith is specifically mentioned (Mk 5:34 and par.; Mt 8:5–13), and at times it is implicitly present (Mk 1:32; Mt 14:36; Lk 5:18–25), there are a significant number of accounts of healings where faith on the part of the sick person is not even implicitly demonstrated (Mk 3:1–6; Mt 12:9–13; Lk 4:33–37; Lk 7:11–17). What seems to be the significant factor is that the healing minister demonstrate a God-experience, a relationship to God which is living and has affected his personality to the extent that we might say he manifests a God-likeness in his person. As one who prays with people for healings, Barbara Shlemon writes:

> When Jesus tells us to ask "in his name," he is teaching us to pray in his personality and character. He wants us to develop the same kind of intimate relationship he had with the Father. . . .This kind of relationship cannot be achieved overnight but requires us to continually immerse ourselves in the personality of Jesus until we become conformed to his image and likeness.[86]

Such an understanding of the significance of a faith relationship seems to be very consistent with biblical healing accounts and would indicate a close connection between the times Jesus went off to be alone with the Father and the encounters he had with people which effected their whole life. The time and effort involved in "putting on the Lord Jesus" might also then be understood as preparation for a healing encounter.

3) The attempt to manifest the personality of Jesus in encounters is a significant part of the healing process, but it seems to demand a certain expectancy on the part of those involved to make the encounter effective. In a recent conference for priests in Steubenville,[87] it became evident to many participants that they had narrowed down the effective power of God's love, not expecting any more than what usually occurs in the sacraments. With regard to the sacrament of reconciliation, Michael Scanlan points out how the expectancy that something will happen is a significant part of making that encounter a healing experience. The same kind of openness to the power of the Spirit of Jesus is significant in making any Christian encounter a healing experience.

While it is clear that one who expects nothing will not be disappointed, it is also evident that too high of an undiscerned expectancy can be harmful. In an article about the divided Christian, Michael Ivens writes about two spiritualities or dispositions toward expectancy which need to balance one another.[88] The spirituality of power, as he calls it, which may tend to expect too much, restores a Christian's faith in expecting grace to be visible, but it runs the danger of projecting one segment of reality, namely, the fact that it has experienced a number of healings, in a generalized way as the whole of reality. It must listen to the facts that some disordered personalities and some physically ill people have not found the cure that they expected; they continued to suffer from their malady after prayer for healing. This spirituality must also be realistic about the fact that there comes a time for people to pass from this life.

The temptation of the spirituality of patience, on the other hand, which expects very little, is to escape into "an inert and evasive peace" like the "terrible peace of the unbeliever," and so it must listen to the spirituality of power "with its stress on the need to meet Christ, to let something happen, to allow oneself to be winkled out of an insulated selfhood by the encouragement and stimulus of the faith community."[89]

Expectancy or openness to the power of God healing in a prayerful encounter is necessary, but it must be in keeping with the realistic facts of life. We can be open to anything happening, realizing the immense power of God's love, but we must express that expectancy in certain situations within the realistic framework of how the love and peace of God has manifested itself throughout Christian history. Most often the minister of healing must be the one to engender in the sick person an openness to the healing effects of the love of God. This is possible without any specific reference to what areas an experience of his love will definitely affect. Though an experienced healer may be able to sense specifically through discernment what result will come, most people might do best to concentrate on manifesting the unselfish love and concern of God in prayer, aware of the many possible healing effects.

4) Another significant element in the healing process is creating an atmosphere for healing, an occasion where the presence of God is made conscious through prayer or singing, where the peace of Jesus fills the air, where one who is in need or ill can feel an unselfish love. Such an

intense healing presence of God was apparently experienced through the personality of Jesus, through the God-presence in him, and it seems that those people throughout Christian history who manifested a God-presence in their personality did effect healings, though perhaps in a lesser intensity. At a conference in Rome in 1975, Father Francis MacNutt spoke of the healing ministry as "bathing a person in Jesus Christ." Agnes Sanford writes that "the essence of all healing is to become so immersed in the being of God that one forgets oneself entirely."[90] Though this being immersed in the presence of God most often happens in interpersonal encounters, it is also understandable how meditation on the passion of Jesus, which manifests his love, or the experience of Jesus in the eucharist, could occasion a healing.

It often seems necessary to have a community of believers who have experienced God to make the "personality of Jesus" manifest to the intensity that it will noticeably effect the healing process, at least for deep injuries or serious illnesses. From the experience of many recent spiritual healing ministers, it is evident that the atmosphere for healing is best created in a praying community. Michael Scanlan writes the following:

Two or more gathered in the name of Jesus brings a special presence of Jesus. It better represents the Body of Jesus and prevents the minister from appropriating the glory to himself. It also multiplies the gifts and ministries that are available. The ministering team is fortified by charismatic gifts of faith, love, discernment of spirits, words of wisdom and knowledge, and prophecy, as well as gifts of compassion, understanding and piety. Even where the minister is forced to be alone because of a sacramental confession, extreme confidentiality of matter, or urgency of time, the minister should consciously identify himself as representing the Body of Christ and where possible seek prayer support. Ideally, the healing will take place in the healing environment of a community of love.[91]

Often to begin the healing process people need an atmosphere where they can "feel secure enough to lay aside the barriers of fear, distrust, and egotism that have shut them off not only from fruitful contact with their fellow human beings but from their own deeper selves."[92] They need to experience the peace of Jesus. It is within small prayer communities that manifest a God-experience which has changed their life, and which they expect can change the lives of others, that most spiritual healing occurs.

93

In visiting a hospital it is not always possible to have a community, but an atmosphere for healing may be created by our own ability to make Jesus present to others, or by bringing to consciousness the healing love that God manifests through the care they receive, or through a community that may be praying for them. Creating such an atmosphere of love and peace, and growing in manifesting the personality of Jesus takes daily effort, even suffering. It requires the effort and pain of transforming our inner dispositions to those of Jesus, the kind of suffering that the New Testament always considered as redemptive.

5) If we have the skills of psychology or are experienced to some extent in the inner workings of the human person, we may help a sick person within the atmosphere of healing, to discover deeper causes or sources of an illness which need to be healed. Such listening and searching may lead to deeper wholeness, or cause a person, who in earlier prayer felt no relief, to experience healing. The minister might ask, especially in praying for inner healing, "What do you think caused the problem, and where did the problem first begin?"[93] Experience has indicated that

praying with people to help them forgive someone or to forgive themselves can effect them on all levels of their person. Matthew Linn writes the following:

> I have seen people shuffle into the psychiatric clinic with long lists of physical symptoms which evaporate one by one as they begin to forgive their parents. I have witnessed many retreatants responding to God's call in ways they never dreamed after they forgave themselves, their neighbor, or God. Especially during the past five years, the Lord has shouted clearly to me that forgiveness brings healing.[94]

While often the need for forgiveness on some level lies at the core of an illness, such forgiveness may be impossible for the person alone, and may need to be made possible by the assurance of the presence of the Lord, the loving support of God's everlasting mercy made conscious through a prayerful confessor or a prayer team.

In healing the past inner hurts of a person's life, or painful memories, the minister of healing may assist people by letting them consciously in thought allow Jesus to walk with them through their past hurts and transform them with his presence. Barbara Shlemon gives an example of a prayer for healing of past hurts:

> Jesus, I ask you to enter into my heart and touch those life experiences which need to be healed .... Wherever you discover the wounded child, touch him, console him, and release him. Walk back through my life to the very moment when I was conceived ... heal any physical or emotional traumas which could have harmed me during the birth process....Jesus, I ask you to surround my infancy with your light and touch those memories which keep me from being free....Walk through my life, Lord, and comfort me when others were not kind. Heal the wounds of encounters which left me frightened, which caused me to retreat into myself and erect barriers to people. ...Thank you Lord.[95]

Though this element of seeking the source of an illness is very important, it may not always be possible or necessary in every situation. Each community of believers, each minister of healing must use the gifts available to manifest the love and mercy of God. Gradually we may become more experienced in the ways of the Lord and be able to discern more precisely what might be best for the one who is sick or injured.

Perhaps the last significant element in a healing encounter is a conscious thankfulness to God for his unlimited healing love. Every healing experience should begin with thanksgiving for the occasion and end in thankfulness for the healing that has begun to happen.

Those "Not Healed"

Though we can examine some of the important factors that might intensify the effects of the healing power of God, the ministry of healing contains too many variables to claim certainty about some questions. If a person is going to manifest the healing power of God to the intensity that people claim noticeable healings through an encounter with him, then people may expect more healings to happen and they may raise the question, "What about those who are prayed with and are not healed?"

The answers to this question have always varied and at times the conclusions drawn have been devastating to those involved. An example of this has been that the minister of healing may say or imply to the sick person that his faith is not strong enough. Such a response grows out of an understanding that if a person has faith he will be healed of anything. Very often this understanding neglects to recognize the many significant factors in the healing process, and it may indicate a misunderstanding of what is meant by faith in the gospels, which was discussed in chapter two.

Some of the current healing ministers have reported that a "lack of healing," at least the healing that was expected, may indicate that there is a deeper source of illness which needs to be made conscious and healed. One example of this mentioned earlier in this chapter is Barbara Shlemon's prayer and discussion with the woman suffering from a bladder infection, while the deeper problem was a lack of forgiveness. The lack of a specific healing in an encounter may be part of leading people to an awareness of the need for a healing at a different level of their person, a healing which may involve a decision on their part to forgive or change a way of relating. A healing may take more time than was first expected.

Some have responded to this question by con-

98

cluding that their suffering from illness must be redemptive. Though it is possible to give value to suffering, as was discussed in chapter five, its value stems from a larger wholeness, a witness to the deeper realities of life. Such a witness gives evidence of a person's having been affected in the orientation of his life by an experience and a relationship to Jesus, which can be part of a healing process.

As we ponder these different responses, we may become aware of the fact that the question raised comes out of a quite mechanical notion of healing where certain activities are expected to produce a predictable result. It also indicates a limited understanding of the human person, presuming that an immediate visible change is the only indication that a prayer for healing was successful. It does not give much credence to the fact that some of the most profound healings take some time, and perhaps more than one encounter.

The question about those who are "not healed" presumes a certain specific expected healing. It may well imply a belief that Jesus healed every person that he met, which would be quite a bit to assume from the limited accounts that were recorded of his life. It would also make us wonder why anyone then would have died during that time.

It is only when we separate visible physical or emotional healing from the larger making whole of the total person, or when we locate the healing power in certain prayers, gestures, or rituals, that we have great difficulty with "those who are not healed." It would seem that the example of Jesus and therefore the mandate to his followers is to manifest a God-like personality, an unselfish love, realizing and consciously proclaiming that such a demonstration of God-with-us has a healing effect. The responsibility of the Christian minister of healing is to occasion healing encounters by lovingly making visible his God-experience which has power to heal.

Summary

The gospel calls us as believers to manifest that healing presence as Jesus did. The intensity of a healing encounter seems to depend to a large extent on the ability of the minister or ministers to let the healing power of God's love flow through them as they encounter one who is ill.

Though the suffering of illness that may derive ultimately from separation from God, or separations among humans, may be given value, such value does not and may not take away from the healing value of manifesting a God-like personality. If indeed it does, then the Christian community and ultimately the whole world is the poorer for it, for the ministry of healing and reconciling is not only a private affair. Michael Scanlan brings this out in his words concerning reconciliation:

> If man can be made whole within himself and reconciled to God, he is then in a position to be an instrument for God to reconcile the world. The emphasis on the power of reconciliation in the sacrament of penance is the necessary beginning of a process of reconciliation in homes, religious communities, institutions, towns, nations, and the world. There is no other place to begin. A man who is not at peace with himself or is not at peace with God cannot bring peace to others.[96]

The healing ministry that accelerates, makes possible, or transcends the natural healing process begins with those who allow God's love to

THE MINISTRY OF HEALING TODAY

take over their personalities. The effects of interiorizing God's healing love and then manifesting that love in relationships are far reaching, limited only by a person's desire to be an instrument of healing to others.

CHAPTER VII

Healing through Suffering

"I have come that you may have life, and have it to the full" (Jn 10:10).

There are certainly other understandings or explanations of healing and suffering, but the view presented in these pages is one that is most consistent with what I have discovered in scripture and in my own experience as confirmed by others presently in the healing ministry. I have not answered all the questions, but perhaps some of the distinctions that I have made will help people answer some of the questions for themselves. My research has pointed out to me new areas in which I need to grow as one who suffers and as one who continues to work toward being a minister of God's healing power. It has given me the assurance that the effort for such growth is worth it.

103

As One Who Suffers

As I mentioned at the beginning, this book stems from real situations of people who are suffering from pain of physical illness or injury, or from the hurt of disrupted emotions, or the pain of spiritual separation or guilt. I have seen and experienced the reality of such pains and have searched and researched to find answers to the questions raised at those times. My searching has confirmed how important it is to have others who care about me in those moments. It has made me recall how comforting and healing it was to have someone who manifested a God-likeness to me, an unselfish, faithful concern for me in times of sickness or injury. A critical look into healings in the New Testament indicates that such encounters are very similar to the way Jesus brought healing, perhaps differing only in the intensity with which he mediated the power of God's faithful love.

During times of pain, it might be difficult to see the value that can be placed on suffering. The reality of the pain may obscure our view of life. Though a conscious recollection of a relationship with Jesus or an encounter with him through a person or event may not always remove all the pain, its effects are usually healing to one seeking wholeness. The hospital patient may come to a peaceful acceptance of the situation and from that vantage point be a minister of healing to a roommate or to a person caring for him. It can be an opportunity to transform the painful realities of human life into a manifestation of the power of God's healing love. The witness of accepted suffering manifests the healing power of Jesus with far-reaching effects. The hospital situation, when faced with openness to the person of Jesus, can lead to healing in many areas.

The understanding of person which indicates the interrelatedness of our activities and illnesses, leads a person who is suffering to seek a healing that will get at the source of an illness and effect a more total health. Through experience I have come to see the value in moments of emotional or spiritual pain. The research for this book has convinced me even more than before of the value of a forgiving encounter with one who can speak forgiveness of sins in the name of Jesus. The realization that the same Jesus of Nazareth cares enough to walk with me through past emotional hurts and fears with the same healing power of love as when he was on earth, has enhanced the healing message of the gospel for me.

As One Who Ministers Healing

Perhaps the most conclusive result of the research that went into this book is to realize that Jesus heals through the abilities of people, through medicine or psychology, or through encounters, by augmenting these abilities or relationships with the power of his love, to the extent that people make him present in those areas. Through abilities surrendered to his service or encounters open to his presence, Jesus can transform the ordinary talents of one's life into means of healing and deeper wholeness. In a prayer community where these or other abilities are put at his service, an encounter with the manifest presence of God can be more intense, and perhaps a richer healing experience can take place.

The research has indicated that there is diversity in how people pray with someone for healing, but each must make manifest the loving presence of God. The most intense spiritual healing experiences which I have read about and experienced have resulted from occasions where the minister or community of ministers mediated a peace and love that can only come from a personal relationship with God. Healing happens through people who manifest a faith relationship with the Lord, an openness to the power of his love, and a humility before him recognizing that they are only instruments of his healing presence. Healing happens where God is intensely present to the sick or injured person who is seeking wholeness. God may be encountered or made consciously present to them by a thought or experience, but often he is most effectively present in the godliness of a human personality, one who freely chooses to transmit him into the actuality of daily life, with the time, effort, and suffering which that involves.

It takes time and effort, and even suffering, to manifest the personality of Jesus to the intensity that will bring healing. It takes the time of continually renewing our relationship to the Lord, continually recalling his attitudes until with his help they become our life dispositions. It takes the effort of seeking out a prayer community that will assist myself and others in deepening our relationship with Jesus until as a team we can mediate a God-likeness to others. It may mean accepting the tension of putting our immediate needs aside, of loving when we are hurting, or forgiving when the pains that an injury caused are not yet erased, of extending ourselves, realizing that we might be rejected or ridiculed.

This project and my limited experience have led me to realize that being a minister of healing is a demanding challenge. We must refine the experiences of personal suffering into compassion for others as Jesus did. It often demands suffering with others, coming into their illness, their pain, and then together, assured by the faithful love of God, being brought to health. It means "being broken for others" that they might be sustained and nourished and brought to full health. It demands effort, but, like Jesus, we must accept the fact that if only "perhaps"[97] someone will be healed, then all the effort is worth it.

The ministry of healing demands stepping out in faith, expecting health in the face of suffering, expecting inner peace in the face of inner turmoil. The healing minister must live with the tension between power and powerlessness, between accepting suffering and claiming Christ's power over it, because "we do the gospel a dis-service if we relax this tension in favor of accept-ing suffering, and forget the promise of Christ to 'do greater works.'"[98] As healing ministers, we must honestly accept the fact that the encounter with Jesus does not and never has removed all suffering. Having accepted that, we must con-tinue to manifest the person of Jesus, realizing the effects that it can have.

While my reading and experience have made me aware of the demands of being a minister of healing, they have also allowed me to feel the reward of such a challenge. There is sustaining comfort in seeing one who was ill being brought to health or one who was hurting being filled with peace through an event or occasion where Christ's power was made present through me. There is something awesome and gratifying about being a direct instrument of the powerful love of God, as Jesus was. George Maloney writes, "Jesus Christ extends his healing love to others through our concrete love toward them. How humbling a thought it is that Jesus heals or does not heal others by the love of God that we allow or fail to radiate out to others."[99]

It is both a challenge and a privilege to accept

the demands of living the personality of Jesus to the extent that we become instruments of God's healing love and peace. No theory of suffering or explanation of healing should deter us from manifesting that love.

Notes

1. John L. McKenzie, "The Son of Man Must Suffer," *The Mystery of Suffering and Death*, ed. Michael J. Taylor, S.J. (New York, 1973), p. 36.
2. McKenzie, p. 37.
3. Notes from a course taught by Father Francis Cleary on "Redemptive Suffering," p. 2.
4. John Bukovsky, "Suffering," *New Catholic Encyclopedia*, XIII (New York, 1967), p. 775.
5. John S. Spong, *This Hebrew Lord* (New York, 1974), p. 99.
6. Spong, p. 105.
7. Joachim Jeremias, "παιφ θεον," *Theological Dictionary of the New Testament*, ed. Gerhard Kittel, V (Grand Rapids, Mich., 1965), p. 715.
8. Jeremias, p. 715.
9. See Spong, Chapter 8 and Clear's notes.
10. Spong, p. 105.
11. Eugene La Verdiere, "Jesus As the Christ in Mark," *New Catholic World*, CCXIX (Nov./Dec. 1976), p. 281.
12. Morton Kelsey, *Healing and Christianity* (New York, N.Y., 1973), p. 89.

13. McKenzie, p. 40.
14. McKenzie, p. 41.
15. Kelsey, p. 362.
16. Albrecht Oepke, "ιαομαι," *Theological Dictionary of the New Testament*, ed. Gerhard Kittel, III (Grand Rapids, Mich., 1965), p. 208.
17. Examples from Hermann Strach and Paul Billerbeck, *Kommentar Zum Neuen Testament*, II (München, 1924).
18. Oepke, p. 208.
19. Rev. Dr. John Wilkinson, "A Study of Healing in the Gospel According to John," *Scottish Journal of Theology*, XX (December 1967), p. 459.
20. Oepke, p. 209.
21. Walter Grundmann, "δυναμαι," *Theological Dictionary of the New Testament*, ed. Gerhard Kittel, II (Grand Rapids, Mich., 1965), p. 302.
22. F. Fenner, *Die Krankheit im Neuen Testament* (1930), p. 96.
23. Fenner, p. 96.
24. Grundmann, p. 302.
25. Oepke, p. 212.
26. Alan Richardson, *The Miracle Stories of the Gospel* (London, 1941), p. 63.
27. Oepke, p. 211.
28. Richardson, p. 63.
29. Oepke, p. 211.
30. Oepke, p. 211.
31. Hermann Beyer, "θεραπεια," *Theological Dictionary of the New Testament*, ed. Gerhard Kittel, III (Grand Rapids, Mich., 1965), p. 130.

32. Beyer, p. 131.
33. Oepke, p. 213.
34. Francis MacNutt, *Healing* (Notre Dame, Indiana, 1974), p. 53.
35. Kelsey, p. 89.
36. Kelsey, p. 124.
37. Oepke, p. 214.
38. Kelsey, p. 124.
39. Grundmann, p. 310.
40. Beyer, p. 131.
41. Grundmann, p. 312.
42. Grundmann, p. 315.
43. Barnabas Mary Ahern, "Fellowship of His Suffering," *The Catholic Biblical Quarterly*, XXII (1960), p. 28.
44. Joseph Blenkinsopp, "We Rejoice in Our Suffering," *The Mystery of Suffering and Death*, ed. Michael Taylor, S.J. (New York, 1973), p. 54.
45. MacNutt, p. 80.
46. Kelsey, p. 149.
47. Kelsey, p. 150.
48. Origen, "Against Celsus," *The Ante-Nicene Fathers*, ed. Rev. Alexander Roberts, D.D. & James Donaldson, LL.d., IV (New York, 1907), p. 473.
49. Kelsey, p. 151.
50. Kelsey, p. 154.
51. Kieran Kavanaugh, "Spirituality," *New Catholic Encyclopedia*, XIII (New York, 1967), p. 595.
52. MacNutt, p. 64.
53. Kelsey, p. 195.
54. Kelsey, p. 195.

55. Kelsey, p. 198.
56. Alfred Rush, "Pope Gregory the Great," *New Catholic Encyclopedia,* VI (New York, 1967), p. 769.
57. Kelsey, p. 203.
58. Adolf Knauber, *Pastoral Theology of Anointing of the Sick* (Collegeville, Minn., 1975), p. 16A.
59. Knauber, p. 18A.
60. Kelsey, p. 209.
61. See the Introduction concerning the main questions.
62. Jürgen Moltmann, *The Crucified God,* (New York, 1974), p. 39.
63. Karl Rahner, *Theological Investigations,* III (Baltimore, Md. 1967), p. 163.
64. Cleary, notes on redemptive suffering.
65. John Hick, "A World Without Suffering," *The Mystery of Suffering and Death,* ed. Michael Taylor, S.J. (New York, 1973), p. 26.
66. Langdon Gilkey, *Maker of Heaven and Earth* (New York, 1959), p. 226.
67. Cleary, notes on redemptive suffering.
68. Gilkey, p. 255.
69. Karl Rahner, *On the Theology of Death* (New York, 1973), p. 44.
70. Karl Rahner, *Theological Investigations* V (Baltimore, Md. 1966), p. 462.
71. Dorothee Soelle, *Suffering* (Philadelphia, Pa., 1975), p. 88.
72. Patricia Lowery, M.M., "The Suffering Servant and The Wounded Healer," *Channel,* XIX (Fall/Winter, 1976), p. 5.

114

73. Lowery, p. 6.
74. Francois H. Lepargneur, O.P., "Sickness in a Christian Anthropology," *The Mystery of Suffering and Death*, ed. Michael Taylor, S.J., (New York, 1973), p. 79.
75. Matthew and Dennis Linn, *Healing of Memories* (New York, 1974), p. 44.
76. Kenneth Pelletier, "Mind as Healer - Mind as Slayer," *Psychology Today*, X (Feb. 1977), p. 35.
77. Kelsey, p. 255.
78. Peter Ford, *The Healing Trinity* (New York, 1971), p. XIV.
79. Michael Scanlan, *Inner Healing* (New York, 1974) p. 12.
80. Barbara Shlemon, *Healing Prayer* (Notre Dame, Ind., 1976), p. 54.
81. Kelsey, p. 359.
82. Julius Weinberger, "The Scientist's Role in Spiritual Healing," *Journal of Pastoral Counseling*, VI (Fall/Winter 1971–72), p. 66.
83. Scanlan, p. 20.
84. Ford, p. 55.
85. MacNutt, p. 120.
86. Shlemon, p. 35.
87. John Haughey, "Healed and Healing Priests," *America*, CXXXIII (Aug. 2, 1975), pp. 46–48.
88. Michael Ivens, "Healing the Divided Self," *The Way*, XVI, (July 1976), pp. 163–175.
89. Ivens, p. 172.
90. Agnes Sanford, *The Healing Light* (Plainfield, N.J., 1947), p. 96.
91. Scanlan, p. 31.

92. MacNutt, p. 156.
93. Michael Scanlan, *The Power in Penance* (Notre Dame, Ind., 1972), p. 36.
94. Linn, p. 2.
95. Shlemon, pp. 82–84.
96. Scanlan, *Penance*, p. 61.
97. "Perhaps"—Jeremiah must recognize that all his efforts cannot force the people of Israel to repent (Jeremiah 26:3; 36:3). God's care and forgiveness of his people, as exemplified in the parable cannot force fruitfulness, yet he continues to care (Lk 13:9).
98. Haughey, p. 48.
99. George Maloney, S.J., *Inward Stillness* (Denville, N.J., 1976), p. 66.

A Selected Bibliography

Ahern, Barnabas Mary, "Fellowship of his Suffering," *The Catholic Biblical Quarterly*, XXII (1960), pp. 1–32.

Benson, Carmen, *What About Us Who Are Not Healed?* Logos International, Plainfield, New Jersey, 1975.

Beyer, Hermann W., "θεραπεια," *Theological Dictionary of the New Testament*, ed. Gerhard Kittel, III, Wm. B. Eerdmann Pub. Co., Grand Rapids, Mich., 1965, pp. 128–132.

Blenkinsopp, Joseph, "We Rejoice in Our Suffering," *The Mystery of Suffering and Death*, ed. Michael J. Taylor, S.J., Alba House, New York, 1973, pp. 45–55.

Bukovsky, John J., "Suffering," *New Catholic Encyclopedia*, XIII, McGraw Hill Company, New York, 1967, pp. 775–776.

Cleary, Fr. Francis, class notes on Redemptive Suffering, 1972.

Fenner, F., *Die Krankheit Im Neuen Testament*, 1930.

Ford, Peter, *The Healing Trinity*, Harper and Row, New York, 1971.

Gilkey, Langdon, *Maker of Heaven and Earth*, Doubleday and Company, Inc., New York, 1959.

A Selected Bibliography

Grundmann, Walter, "δυναμαι," *Theological Dictionary of the New Testament*, Ed. Gerhard Kittel, II, Wm. B. Eerdman Publ, Co., Grand Rapids, Mich., 1965, pp. 284–317.

Hick, John "A World Without Suffering," *The Mystery of Suffering and Death*, ed. Michael J. Taylor, S.J., Alba House, New York, 1973, pp. 25–30.

Hick, John, *Evil and the God of Love*, Lowe and Brydone Ltd., Norfolk, England, 1966.

Ivens, Michael, "Healing the Divided Self," *The Way*, XVI (July 1976), pp. 163–175.

Jeremias, Joachim, "παιϕ θεον," *Theological Dictionary of the New Testament*, ed. Gerhard Kittel, V, Wm. B. Eerdman Pub. Co., Grand Rapids, Mich., 1965, pp. 654–716.

Jerome Biblical Commentary, ed. Raymond Brown, S.S. et al., Prentice-Hall, Inc., New Jersey, 1968.

Kavanaugh, Kieran, "Spirituality," *New Catholic Encyclopedia*, XII, McGraw Hill Company, New York, 1967, pp. 594–598.

Kelsey, Morton, *Healing and Christianity*, Harper and Row, New York, 1973.

Knauber, Dr. Adolf, *Pastoral Theology of the Anointing of the Sick*, Liturgical Press, Collegeville, Minn., 1975.

La Verdiere, Eugene, "Jesus As the Christ in Mark," *New Catholic World*, CCXIX (Nov./Dec. 1976), pp. 277–281.

Lepargneur, O. P., Francois H., "Sickness in a Christian Anthropology," *The Mystery of Suffering and Death*, ed. Michael J. Taylor, S.J., Alba House, New York, 1973, pp. 71–80.

A Selected Bibliography

Lewis, C. S., *The Problem of Pain*, MacMillan Co., New York, 1944.

Linn, Matthew and Dennis, *Healing of Memories*, Paulist Press, New York, 1974.

Lowery, M.M., Patricia, "The Suffering Servant and the Wounded Healer," *Channel*, XIX (Fall/Winter 1976), pp. 4–8.

MacNutt, O. P., Francis, *Healing*, Ave Maria Press, Notre Dame, Ind., 1974.

Maloney, S. J., George, *Inward Stillness*, Dimension Books, Denville, New Jersey, 1976.

McKenzie, John L., "The Son of Man Must Suffer," *The Mystery of Suffering and Death*, ed. Michael J. Taylor, S.J., Alba House, New York, 1973, pp. 31–44.

Moltmann, Jürgen, *The Crucified God*, Harper and Row, New York, 1974.

New American Bible, Thomas Nelson Inc., New York, 1971.

Oepke, Albrecht, "ιαομαι," *Theological Dictionary of the New Testament*, ed. Gerhard Kittel, III, Wm. B. Eerdman Pub. Co., Grand Rapids, Mich., 1965, pp. 194–215.

Origen, "Against Celsus," *The Ante-Nicene Fathers*, ed. Rev. Alexander Roberts, D.D., and James Donaldson, LL.D., IV, Charles Scribner Sons, New York, 1907, pp. 395–669.

Pelletier, Kenneth, "Mind as Healer—Mind as Slayer," *Psychology Today*, X (Feb. 1977), pp. 35–40, 82–88.

Rahner, Karl, *On the Theology of Death*, Seabury Press, New York, 1973.

A Selected Bibliography

Rahner, Karl, *Theological Investigations*, III, Helican Press, Baltimore, Md., 1967.

Rahner, Karl, *Theological Investigations*, V, Helicon Press, Baltimore, Md., 1966.

Richardson, Alan, *The Miracle Stories of the Gospel*, S.C.M. Press, LTD., London, England, 1941.

Rush, Alfred, "Pope Gregory the Great," *New Catholic Encyclopedia, VI*, McGraw Hill Company, New York, 1967, pp. 766–770.

Sanford, Agnes, *The Healing Light*, Logos International, Plainfield, New Jersey, 1947.

Scanlan, Michael, *Inner Healing*, Paulist Press, New York, 1974.

Scanlan, Michael, *The Power in Penance*, Ave Maria Press, Notre Dame, Ind., 1972.

Schillebeeckx, O. P., Edward, *Christ, the Sacrament of the Encounter with God*, Sheed and Ward, New York, 1963.

Shlemon, Barbara, "Healing of the Inner Man," *New Covenant*, III, (May 1974), pp. 7–10.

Shlemon, Barbara, *Healing Prayer*, Ave Maria Press, Notre Dame, Ind., 1972.

Soelle, Dorothee, *Suffering*, Fortress Press, Philadelphia, Pa., 1975.

Spong, John S., *This Hebrew Lord*, Seabury Press, New York, 1974.

Strack, Hermann, and Billerbeck, Paul, *Kommentar Zum Neuen Testament*, II, C.H. Becksche Verlags-Buchhandlung, München, 1924.

Sutcliff, S.J., Edmund, *Providence and Suffering in the Old and New Testament*, Thomas Nelson and Sons Ltd., New York, 1953.

A Selected Bibliography

Theology of Atonement, ed. John Sheets, S.J., Prentice-Hall Inc., New Jersey, 1967.

Tyrrell, Bernard, *Christotherapy*, Seabury Press, New York, 1975.

Weinberger, Julius, "The Scientist's Role in Spiritual Healing," *Journal of Pastoral Counseling*, VI (Fall/Winter 1971–72), pp. 64–67.

Wilkinson, Dr. John, "A Study of Healing in the Gospel According to John," *Scottish Journal of Theology*, XX (Dec. 1967), pp. 442–461.

121